Understanding Wall Street

By Jeffrey B. Little and Lucien Rhodes

First printing: May, 1978
Second printing: November, 1978
Third printing: January, 1980
Fourth printing: October, 1980
Fifth printing: April, 1981
Sixth printing: September, 1981
Seventh printing: February, 1982
Eighth printing: July, 1982
Ninth printing: October, 1982

P9-CEJ-814

LIBERTY PUBLISHING COMPANY
Cockeysville, Maryland

Published by:
  Liberty Publishing Company, Inc.
  50 Scott Adam Road
  Cockeysville, Maryland 21030

Library of Congress #78-54787

ISBN #0-89709-010-1

Manufactured USA

Understanding Wall Street

Table of Contents

Over the years, the public has been encouraged to "Own a Share of America." Yet, how many individuals have been prepared to invest wisely?

The stock market is rarely taught in high school, and even on the college level, investment courses are typically selected only by students with specialized business interests. Moreover, investors have found it difficult to educate themselves, even with the flood of literature available to date. Free pamphlets and superficial guides have not provided substance, encyclopedic texts have been too intimidating, and the "get-rich-quick" books have deluded investors with false hopes of easy gains.

Understanding Wall Street provides a good, practical education by combining investment fundamentals and many sophisticated techniques. It was written for two readers: first, the individual who knows little or nothing about the stock market but has always wanted to understand it; and second, the "experienced" investor who recognizes there is much more to learn. Therefore, this book includes more than just a history of Wall Street or how to read the stock tables. It also describes, for example, the reinvestment rate and the computation of current equity in a short seller's margin account.

Understanding Wall Street is the bound edition of THE WALL STREET LIBRARY, a nine-volume series. Each chapter is an independent unit of study and all nine chapters together form a complete educational program.

What is a share of stock?

Introduction Every business day millions of shares of stock are bought and sold. How did these shares originate and how are the prices determined? For shares to be traded from one person to another, a company must be created. How does it begin? Where does the money come from?

In this chapter, the New Design Chair Company is born and its officers confront the problems all successful corporations must solve. Directors are elected, shares are issued, profits are reinvested into the business and dividends are declared. In the process, the reader sees capitalism at work.

The chapter concludes with a Wall Street dictionary that explains widely used terms and expressions.

The New-Design Chair Company Charlie, a young inventor, has just built a new folding chair having a superior design. Encouraged by family and friends, he decides to turn his hobby of building chairs into a full-time business rather than sell his patents to a large chair company.

Although Charlie has savings that could be put into the venture, the amount is far short of the total capital necessary. He estimates the total cost of the factory, machinery and initial money needed for product inventory to be approximately $2 million.

These "assets" (the factory, machinery, inventory and remaining capital) would be used to produce the chairs. The more chairs Charlie can produce using these assets, the more profitable the business would be.

Charlie calculates that if he could make and sell at least 100,000 chairs annually, it would cost about $20 to manufacture each chair. In addition, he estimates the sales and marketing expenses for each chair to be roughly $10. Since each new chair would be sold to his customers at the competitive price of $35, his profit (before paying federal, state and local taxes) would be $5 per chair.

— One Chair —

	Selling Price	$35.00
Less	Cost of Wood and Materials, Salaries, Labor, Other Direct Costs	20.00
	"Gross Profit"	**$15.00**
Less	Advertising Expenses, Sales Commissions, Other Expenses	10.00
	Profit Before Taxes	**$ 5.00**

Charlie believes his new enterprise would be beneficial in several ways. Thousands would enjoy using the new chairs, many people in his community would be earning a living by making and selling the chairs, and the business would also contribute to the welfare of his community, state and country through the payment of taxes. If Charlie could, indeed, manufacture and sell 100,000 chairs, this activity would no longer be a hobby. It would be a sizable business:

— 100,000 Chairs —

	Total Sales	$3,500,000
Less	Cost of Wood and Materials, Salaries, Labor, Other Direct Costs	2,000,000
	"Gross Profit"	$1,500,000
Less	Advertising Expenses, Sales Commissions, Other Expenses	1,000,000
	Profit Before Taxes	$ 500,000
Less	Federal, State, Local Taxes	240,000
	Net Profit or "Earnings"	$ 260,000

Now Charlie faces a major problem. Where will he get almost $2 million for the factory, machinery and working capital? He is unable to borrow such a large amount without collateral.

He decides to find others, frequently called "venture capitalists," who might also see the potential for his idea and be willing to risk some capital to get the venture started. To interest others, Charlie must divide his new business into smaller pieces to give them some ownership. Charlie realizes, too, that by relinquishing some ownership, he would no longer be entitled to all the profits from the manufacture of the chairs. However, he is willing to do this to secure the help of others.

After exploring the advantages and disadvantages of the various legal forms of businesses, he decides to establish a "corporation." The principal reason for choosing a corporation rather than a partnership or any other form was *financial liability*. Charlie learned that no matter which legal structure is used, creditors always have first claim on the assets if the business fails. However, a corporation, as a legal entity, limits the financial risk of the owners to the amount of capital invested. In other words, stockholders of a corporation are not liable for more than they invest.

Charlie forms the corporation under the laws of the state, names it the New-Design Chair Company, and selects a few individuals to act as the board of directors until the Company's first annual meeting of stockholders. At that time, a board of directors will be formally elected by the stockholders. The directors decide to "issue" 250,000 *shares* of stock of the 400,000 total possible shares authorized by the company's founding charter (when the company was organized this was the number of shares determined to be the most convenient and practical for the company's needs). The 250,000 shares are divided between Charlie and the venture capitalists in proportion to their agreed ownership determined by the contribution of

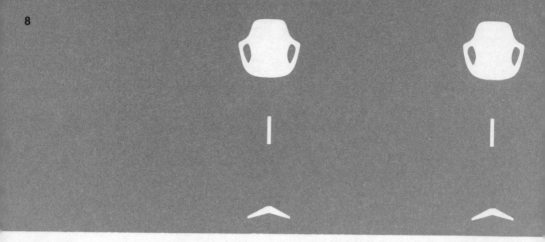

each. Charlie, of course, still owns a meaningful amount because of his importance to the company, his chair patents and his initial capital. Now it can be said they are "stockholders in common."

Each stockholder is a part owner in the company, although the extent of ownership depends upon the number of shares held (an individual who holds 50 shares of the total 250,000 shares issued owns 1/5000th of the entire company whereas a person who has 10,000 shares owns 1/25th of the company). The remaining 150,000 shares might be issued by the directors at a later date if the company finds it necessary. However, at the present time, the company's ownership is divided into 250,000 pieces. In other words, there are currently 250,000 shares outstanding of 400,000 shares authorized.

The members of the board of directors, including Charlie, are elected by the stockholders to oversee the affairs of the company. Each share outstanding, according to the company's charter, is entitled to an equal vote in the annual election of the directors.

Most of the needed $2 million has been contributed in the form of "equity capital" by the venture capitalists. To raise the remaining capital, the company decides to go into debt. If the company were to borrow this money expecting to pay it back in a relatively short period of time, a bank could be approached for a loan. If, on the other hand, a longer time period is needed, the company might consider selling *bonds*.

The New-Design Chair Company, being a young, unproven business, would probably be unable to issue bonds solely on its word or good name (if it could, bonds of this type would be called "debentures"). Lenders are usually reluctant to loan money to a new firm without security. Consequently, the New-Design Chair Company might be asked to put up some property as collateral (bonds of this type are often called "mortgage bonds").

Although the New-Design Chair Company would have to pay interest on the money it borrows, present stockholders would not have to give up ownership as Charlie did when the new stock was issued for equity capital. On the other hand, the lenders (bondholders) have first claim on the company's property if the company fails to repay the debt (called a "default").

The Importance of Profits Why did Charlie and his associates risk their personal savings to build a factory to manufacture the chairs? They could have put their money into a savings bank rather than into the new enterprise. The money would have been safe and the bank would have paid them interest. Why would *anybody* be willing to risk money — let alone $2 million — to start the New-Design Chair Company? The answer is simple: PROFITS.

Charlie and his associates saw an opportunity to make a meaningful profit on each chair manufactured if the company met its business objectives. The stockholders also saw the possibility of increasing their profits in later years if more chairs could be manufactured and sold. In short, Charlie and his associates figured they could achieve a much better return on their money by investing in the new venture rather than receiving interest from the bank.

Now time has passed, Charlie's projections were accurate, and the venture has been successful. According to the statement of income in its recent annual report to stockholders, the New Design Chair Company sold 100,000 chairs last year resulting in a net profit, also called earnings, of $260,000 — just as Charlie antici-pated. The stockholders of the company are now entitled to divide this money among themselves. Since there are 250,000 shares outstanding, dividing the earnings of $260,000 equally means that, for every share held, a stockholder would be entitled to $1.04 per share ($260,000 divided by 250,000 shares). *This calculation is called earnings per share.* If, next year or the year after, the New-Design Chair Company increases its production of chairs and earns, for example, $500,000, the earnings per share calculation would be $2.00 per share ($500,000 divided by 250,000 shares).

Each year the directors of the company must decide what to do with the earnings. If the company were to distribute to its stockholders part or all of last year's $260,000 earnings, this cash payment would be called a "dividend." The size of the dividend declared by the directors each year would most likely be determined by the amount of profits available. However, regardless of the total amount declared, each share would receive an equal dividend. The stockholder owning a greater number of shares would, of course, receive a larger dividend check from the company.

The directors of the New-Design Chair Company might decide to declare only a small dividend or maybe none at all. If most or all of the $260,000 net profit is used to increase the size of the factory, hire more people or add to the company's research program to design better chairs, the stockholders might enjoy higher earnings and bigger dividends in later years without having to invest any additional capital. This process is called "internal financing."

At the board meeting the directors declare a dividend of $0.26 per share or a total of $65,000 (one-fourth of the earnings). In effect, the $0.26 per share dividend represents a 25% payout of the $1.04 earnings per share. The remaining $195,000 not paid out will be reinvested back into the business. These "retained earnings" will also enhance the company's financial condition which is expressed by a balance sheet in the annual report. The balance sheet shows what the company *owns,* what it *owes* and the value of the remaining amount called *stockholders' equity* (i.e., the net worth of the stockholders' ownership).

Obviously stockholders of the New-Design Chair Company will be watching the company's earnings progress closely. As they examine their company's profitability, they will be asking two basic questions:
• How much profit was produced by each sales dollar?
• How much profit was produced by each dollar of stockholders' equity?

The typical U.S. company today earns only 5% or about 5 cents profit after taxes from each sales dollar. This profit also represents approximately 13-14% of each dollar of stockholders' equity.

Clearly, profits are important to *everyone* in our economic system. Without profits to spur individual initiative and encourage investment, factories would not be built, people would not be using better products and many more workers would be looking for employment.

The Stock Price Once a company's stock has been issued and is outstanding, how is the market price determined? To answer this question, there is an old Wall Street saying: "A stock is only worth what someone is willing to pay." Although the saying is somewhat shortsighted, there is some truth to it. A stockholder wanting to sell his shares in the New-Design Chair Company, for example, could sell for no more than the price someone else would be willing to pay. The stock is rarely sold back to the company since the company's financial resources are tied up in the business. If the firm is prospering and the outlook is bright, there could be many eager investors ready to buy the shares at the asking price or maybe higher. A large demand to buy would mean higher bids for the stock. On the other hand, if the outlook for the business is unfavorable, an anxious buyer might be scarce. Perhaps the asking price would have to be reduced to attract buyers. It is simply the supply/demand situation at that moment.

There are many factors an investor must consider when estimating a value for the stock. However, generally speaking, an investor is most interested in the company's *earnings outlook, dividend prospects* and *financial condition.* The stock price revolves around these three fundamental factors as investors compare the stock to all other investment opportunities.

Two Wall Street terms used frequently to appraise stocks are "Price/Earnings Ratio" and "Dividend Yield." They are not as complicated as they sound.

Price/Earnings Ratio

The "P/E ratio," or "P/E multiple" as it is also called, simply describes the relationship between the stock price and the earnings per share. It is easily calculated by dividing the price of the stock by the earnings per share figure. For example, if the price of the stock happens to be $30 and the annual earnings per share is $1.50, the P/E ratio is 20 ($30 divided by $1.50 per share).

Dividend Yield

The dividend yield, or often just referred to as "yield," represents the annual percent return that the dividend provides. The yield of a stock is calculated by dividing the annual cash dividend per share by the price of the stock. For example, if a company pays its stockholders an annual cash dividend of $0.60 per share and the stock price happens to be $30, the return, or dividend yield, is 2.0% ($0.60 per share divided by $30).

"There are two requirements for success in Wall Street. One, you have to think correctly; and secondly, you have to think independently."

— Benjamin Graham

Although a low P/E ratio is considered desirable, it is a common mistake to automatically assume that a stock having a low P/E ratio is more attractively priced than another stock having a higher P/E. A stock with a P/E ratio of 8 times, for example, is not necessarily a better value than one with a P/E multiple of, say, 20 times earnings if future profits of the first company grow much more slowly, or maybe not at all, compared with the second company. A higher P/E ratio implies, but does not necessarily mean, greater investment risk.

The same applies to the dividend yield. A stock paying a dividend that yields a return of, say, 7.0% is not necessarily more attractive than another stock with a lower dividend yield of 2.0%, for example. How secure or safe is the dividend? What is the chance that the dividend will be increased in the future? How much of the earnings is being paid out as a cash dividend to shareholders rather than being reinvested back into the business for future growth? These and other related questions must be considered.

Of course the P/E ratio and the dividend yield never remain constant. The P/E ratio increases and the dividend yield declines when the stock price moves higher. Conversely, the P/E ratio declines and the dividend yield increases when the stock price goes down. Moreover, the P/E ratio and dividend yield will also vary as the company's earnings and dividends increase or decrease.

Over a period of days, weeks or months, the price of a stock can fluctuate widely depending upon the direction of the overall stock market or news items affecting the company or its industry. Sometimes a stock will rise or fall for no apparent reason. Any number of circumstances or events can influence the confidence level of investors and the supply/demand balance of buyers and sellers. However, over an extended time period — a few years or longer — the stock price will most likely rise or fall in line with the company's earnings, dividends and financial condition.

Why Do People Buy Stocks? Where should that extra money go? Into the savings bank? Bonds? Real estate? Art? Or will the stock market provide the best possible return? While each individual has a different investment objective, stocks are bought for one primary reason: *to make money*.

An Hour with Mr. Graham
The Financial Analysts Research
Foundation, 1977.

13

An individual can participate in the stock market in three ways:

Investing

This is generally the most successful approach because time can be used to an advantage. An *investor* buys shares to be a part owner of the company and to obtain at least an adequate return on the investment (i.e., enough to justify the risk and enable the investor to keep ahead of the rising cost of living). The investment time horizon is usually a few years or longer.

Speculating

The *speculator* is willing to assume great risk for a potentially great reward. Being a part owner is not important to the speculator since the time horizon is to be no longer than necessary.

Trading

A *trader* attempts to take advantage of small price changes and is less interested in intrinsic value. Stock certificates are merely pieces of paper to be bought or sold for a profit within a short period of time — sometimes days or hours.

Whether investing, speculating or trading, a stockholder makes money by receiving *cash dividends* (usually paid quarterly) from the company and/or by obtaining *capital appreciation* if the stock is sold at a higher price than the original purchase price. Each day the stockholder can calculate the theoretical profit or loss on a piece of paper (hence the terms "paper profit" and "paper loss") but a profit or loss is not, as they say, "realized" until the stock is actually sold.

The stock market can be different things to different people. An older person, for example, might invest in stocks with an objective of obtaining a high, but fairly secure, dividend yield. A middle-aged couple might prefer buying only high quality stocks with an investment objective of growth and modest dividend returns. A young investor, on the other hand, might not be interested in a current dividend return. Instead, he or she might be willing to assume greater risk and buy shares of small, rapidly growing companies for maximum capital appreciation. In any case, it is particularly important for an investor to use only as much stock market capital as he or she can safely afford, to identify an investment objective and to know what to expect from each dollar invested.

Dictionary of Wall Street

annual meeting A stockholder meeting, normally held at the same time each year, to elect the company's board of directors and transact other business.

arbitrage The practice of buying and selling two separate but related securities to profit from the difference in their values. An arbitrage opportunity often arises when two companies plan to merge or when one security is convertible into another.

asset Anything of value owned by a company. Assets can include cash, product inventory and other current assets, as well as land, buildings, equipment, etc.

authorized See "shares authorized."

averaging down The purchase of additional shares of a stock already owned at lower prices to reduce the average cost per share of all shares held.

balance sheet A financial statement showing the company's assets (what the company owns), its liabilities (what it owes), and the difference, called "net worth" or "stockholders' equity."

bear market A declining trend in stock prices occurring usually in a time period of months or years.

beta The second letter of the Greek alphabet — used by Wall Street to describe the volatility of a stock relative to a stock market index. Beta is regarded by some as a measure of stock market risk.

block A large amount of stock sold as a single unit. The term is most often used to describe a unit of 1,000 shares or more.

blue sky laws State laws designed to protect investors from "blue sky" (worthless) securities.

board of directors A group of people elected, usually annually, by the stockholders to exercise powers granted by the corporation's charter. These powers could include appointments of officers, issuance of shares, declaration of dividends, etc.

bond A certificate of indebtedness extending over a period of more than one year from the time it is issued. A debt of less than one year is usually called a "note." A bond is an obligation that must be repaid at a certain time. Meanwhile, the borrower pays interest to the bondholder for the use of the money.

book value The equity value of an outstanding share of stock. Book value is determined by dividing the amount of stockholders' equity to which each share is entitled by the number of shares outstanding.

broad tape A news service used by brokerage firms and other business offices. The service provides a continuous printed stream of current business news items. The news is printed on a "broad tape" of paper.

bull market A rising trend in stock prices generally occurring within a time period of months or years.

call option A contract giving the holder a right to buy 100 shares of a stock at a predetermined price (called the striking price) any time up to a predetermined expiration date.

capital gain A gain realized on the sale or exchange of securities, fixed property or similar assets. The gain, which is taxable, can be either long term or short term depending upon the length of time the asset is held.

capital loss A loss realized on the sale or exchange of securities, fixed property or similar assets. The loss can sometimes be used to reduce taxes.

capitalism A profit-oriented economic system involving the private ownership of production and distribution in a competitive environment.

capitalization All money that has been invested in the business including equity capital (common stock and preferred stock), long term debt (bonds), retained earnings and other surplus funds.

cash flow Loosely defined as "net income plus depreciation." The term is frequently used to describe the amount of internally-generated cash available for dividends and/or for the purchase of additional assets.

closed-end fund An investment company with a limited number of shares. To buy or sell, a shareholder must buy from or sell to another person rather than dealing directly with the investment company.

conglomerate A broadly diversified corporation encompassing products in many unrelated industries. Rightly or wrongly, the term connotes a lack of corporate direction.

convertible debenture A debenture that is convertible into common shares at the option of the owner.

convertible preferred stock A preferred stock that is convertible into common shares at the option of the owner.

corner Such complete supply/demand control of a security that its price can be manipulated. The practice is illegal today and the term is primarily historic.

coupon A promise to pay interest when due and is usually attached to a bond. When the due date arrives, the coupon is detached and submitted for payment. The term also refers to a bond's interest rate.

current assets Assets that are expected to be converted to cash within twelve months.

current liabilities Obligations that will be paid within twelve months.

current ratio The ratio of current assets to current liabilities. The current ratio is calculated by dividing current assets by current liabilities. Current assets at least twice current liabilities is considered a healthy condition for most businesses.

debenture An unsecured (without collateral) bond issued on the good word and general credit of the borrower.

deflation The economic condition of falling prices for goods and services. Deflation, the inverse to inflation, refers to the increasing buying power of cash and a substantially reduced amount of currency in circulation.

depreciation The estimated decrease in value of property due to use, deterioration or obsolescence over a period of time. Although depreciation does not require a cash outlay, it is a cost of doing business.

dividend A payment to stockholders, usually in the form of a quarterly check. The dividend is declared by the board of directors and is normally determined by the level of the company's earnings.

discount The amount below the list price or face value. A bond discount refers to the excess of the face value over its current market price. A bond that sells below 100, or par, is said to be "selling at a discount."

dollar-cost-averaging An investment approach that involves consistently buying uniform dollar amounts of a security regardless of the price. When prices are low more shares are bought than when prices are high.

dual listing The same security listed on more than one exchange.

earned surplus Another term for "retained earnings."

earnings The amount of profit a company realizes after all costs, expenses and taxes have been paid. See also: "net earnings."

earnings per share The net earnings divided by the average shares outstanding.

equity See "stockholders' equity."

financing The sale of new stock or bonds by a corporation for the purpose of raising capital.

float The number of shares currently available for trading. The float is calculated by deducting, from the shares outstanding, the number of shares closely held by individuals or institutions not likely to sell immediately if the stock price rises.

fundamentalist One who believes that stock prices are determined by the future course of earnings and dividends. The fundamentalist studies, among other things, economics, industry conditions and corporate financial statements.

going public A term used to describe the sale of shares of a privately-held company to the public for the first time.

gross profits Profits earned from the basic manufacturing or service operation — before selling costs and other expenses are deducted and before taxes are paid.

income statement A financial statement that presents a company's business results over a specific period of time, usually quarterly or annually. It shows, in dollar terms, all revenues, costs and expenses, taxes and earnings.

inflation The economic condition of rising prices for goods and services. Inflation refers to a declining buying power of cash and a substantially greater amount of currency in circulation. It is generally the result of excessive government spending.

insider An officer or director of a company or another person having corporate information not available to the public.

institutional investor A bank, mutual fund, pension fund, insurance company, university or other institution that invests in the securities markets.

interest The compensation a borrower pays a lender for the use of money borrowed.

interim report A company report, usually quarterly, that presents a company's business results (income statement) for the period and, sometimes, the current financial condition (balance sheet). During the year a company will normally issue three interim reports and one annual report.

liability Anything a company owes. Liabilities can include current liabilities as well as debt to be repaid in later years (e.g., bonds).

liquidate The action of selling assets or securities to obtain cash.

liquidity The ability of a stock to absorb a large amount of buying or selling without disturbing the price substantially.

load mutual fund An open-end investment company that charges the investor a fee when the investor buys the fund shares. This fee (or "load", as it is called) is used primarily to compensate salesmen selling the fund.

long term The length of time a stock or bond must be held to qualify for a more favorable tax rate. Until recent tax law revisions, "long term" meant six months or more. Beginning in 1978, "long term" will be a holding period of one year or more.

long term debt Liabilities that are expected to be repaid after twelve months.

margin account An account, typically with a brokerage firm, that allows an investor to buy or sell securities on credit. An investor can sometimes borrow up to 50% or more of the investment value.

market breadth The extent or scope of change in stock prices. Market breadth is most often measured by analyzing the number of stocks that advanced or declined during the period or by counting the number of stocks hitting new highs or new lows.

market order An order to buy or sell at the best possible price as soon as it can be accomplished.

municipal bond A bond issued by a state, territory, or possession of the United States or by any municipality, political subdivision or agency. Included are bonds issued by cities, counties, school districts, authorities, etc.

mutual fund An open-end investment company. A mutual fund offers the investor the benefits of portfolio diversification (i.e., owning more shares to provide greater safety and reduce volatility).

NASDAQ *(pronounced "nazdak")* The computerized National Association of Securities Dealers Automatic Quotation system that provides brokers and dealers with price quotations of securities traded over-the-counter.

net earnings or net income or net profit The profit a company realizes after all costs, expenses and taxes have been paid. See also: "earnings."

net profit margin The profitability of a company after taxes are paid. The net profit margin is calculated by dividing net earnings by total revenues (sales and other income).

net worth See "stockholders' equity."

no-load mutual fund An open-end investment company that allows investors to buy and sell fund shares without paying a fee (called the "load"). A no-load fund is sold by word-of-mouth since it typically has no salesmen.

odd lot Any number of shares less than a round lot. Normally, an odd lot is 1 to 99 shares with a round lot being 100 shares or a multiple of 100 shares.

odd lot differential A small, extra charge an investor pays if an odd lot is purchased. The amount is ordinarily ⅛ of a point per share.

open-end investment company An investment company that uses its capital to invest in other companies. Its shareholders can participate directly because the open-end investment company will sell or rebuy its own shares at book value. See also: "mutual fund."

open order An order still pending or on the books to buy or sell a security, but not yet executed. An open order will remain in effect until it is either executed or cancelled.

operating profit The profit a company earns from operations before taxes are paid. It is the remainder after deducting all operating costs from sales.

operating profit margin The profitability of a company's operations before taxes are paid. The operating profit margin is calculated by dividing operating profits by sales.

option A contract allowing an investor to purchase or sell 100 shares of a stock at a predetermined price any time up to a predetermined expiration date.

outstanding See "shares outstanding."

over-the-counter The nationwide network of brokers/dealers engaged in buying and selling securities that, for the most part, are not listed on exchanges.

paper profit A profit that has not been realized. In most cases, the term "paper profit" refers to the profit an investor has on a security that was purchased earlier but has not yet been sold.

par value In bonds, par value refers to the stated value of a bond (usually $1,000 or 100). In stocks, par value is an arbitrary value primarily used for bookkeeping purposes.

payout ratio The proportionate amount of a company's earnings paid out to stockholders as a dividend. For example, a company that pays a $0.25 dividend out of every $1.00 of earnings has a payout ratio of 25%.

pink sheets A daily list of over-the-counter stocks not traded on NASDAQ and the broker/dealers making markets in them. The pink sheets normally show the bid and asked prices of the prior day.

preferred stock A stock that has prior claim on dividends (and/or assets in the case of corporate dissolution) up to a certain amount before the common stockholders are entitled to anything.

premium The amount above the list price or face value. A bond premium refers to the excess of the market price over its face value. A bond that sells above 100, or par, is said to be "selling at a premium."

pretax margin The profitability of a company before taxes are paid. The pretax margin is calculated by dividing pretax profits by total revenues (sales and other income).

pretax profits The profit a company earns before paying taxes. It is the remainder after deducting all costs and expenses other than taxes from total revenues.

price/earnings ratio or **P/E ratio** The relationship between the price of a stock and its earnings per share. The P/E ratio is calculated by dividing the stock price by the earnings per share figure. A stock selling at $45 with earnings of $3.00 per share has a price/earnings ratio of 15.

private placement A stock or bond issue that is sold by a company directly to an investor or a group of investors without involving an underwriter or registration with the SEC.

profit margin The profitability of a company measured by relating profits to revenues. The three most common profit margin calculations are: operating profit margin, pretax profit margin and net profit margin.

prospectus A document issued by a corporation at the time securities are offered providing buyers or potential buyers with pertinent details and data on the corporation and the security being issued.

proxy A written authorization by a stockholder allowing a representative or someone else to vote for or against directors and business proposals at the annual meeting. The results of these votes are usually announced at the meeting.

proxy fight Two or more groups soliciting signed proxies from stockholders to gain a voting majority. Usually it is to win control of the corporation and oust the incumbent management.

put option A contract giving the holder the right to sell 100 shares of a stock at a predetermined price (called the striking price) any time up to a predetermined expiration date.

quick-asset ratio or **acid-test ratio** Current assets less inventories as a percent of current liabilities (i.e., current assets - inventories divided by current liabilities). Some accounting experts prefer dividing the sum of cash and marketable securities by current liabilities. A company's position is considered healthy when quick assets exceed current liabilities.

random walk A stock market theory based on the belief that stock price movements are completely random and unpredictable.

red herring A preliminary prospectus easily identified because much of the cover is printed in red as a warning to investors that the document is not complete or final.

retained earnings Earnings that have been reinvested back into the business after dividends are paid to stockholders. Retained earnings is often an important component of a company's stockholders' equity. Another name for retained earnings is "earned surplus".

retention rate The percent of net earnings available for reinvestment into the company after dividends are paid to stockholders. The retention rate is also the inverse of the payout ratio. If the payout ratio is 25%, the retention rate is 75%.

return on equity The rate of investment return a company earns on stockholders' equity. Return on equity is calculated by dividing net earnings by average stockholders' equity.

reinvestment rate The internal growth potential of a company. The reinvestment rate is calculated by multiplying the company's return on equity by the retention rate.

revenues or **total revenues** A term used loosely to describe the income sources of a corporation (i.e., sales and other income) before any costs or expenses are deducted.

round lot A standard unit of trading or a multiple thereof. Generally speaking, the unit of trading is 100 shares in the case of stocks and $1,000 par value in the case of bonds.

19

sales The total dollar value of products sold. It is the number of units sold multiplied by the sales price per unit.

secondary A large block of stock purchased by a securities firm or a group of firms for resale, usually in smaller lots at a fixed price. The shares are purchased from existing stockholders (not from the company).

SEC The Securities and Exchange Commission, established by Congress to administer the Securities Act of 1933 and several other investment-related acts.

senior securities Bonds and/or preferred stocks within the capitalization of a corporation. These securities are considered "senior" to the common stock.

settlement date The date on which money or securities are due once securities have been purchased or sold (five business days after the trade date).

shares authorized The maximum number of shares allowed to be issued under a corporation's charter. Additional shares require a charter amendment.

shares outstanding The number of authorized shares that have been issued and are now in the hands of owners.

short "against the box" A short sale involving stock that is already owned (rather than borrowing it). This trading technique is used primarily for tax reasons.

short interest Shares that have been sold short but not yet repurchased.

short sale A trading technique typically used when a stock is expected to decline in price. A short sale involves selling borrowed stock anticipating that the same number of shares will be repurchased later at a lower price.

short term The length of time a stock or bond is held before it becomes a long term investment. Traditionally, "short term" meant less than six months. Beginning in 1978, "short term" will be a holding period up to one year.

sinking fund An arrangement whereby a portion of a bond or preferred stock issue is retired periodically prior to its fixed maturity date.

statement of income See "Income Statement."

stock dividend A dividend paid in securities rather than cash.

stock split A division of a company's shares into a greater or lesser number.

stockholders' equity The difference between a company's total assets and total liabilities. Stockholders' equity, sometimes called "net worth," is the stockholders' ownership in the company.

"stop-loss order" or "stop order" An order that becomes a "market order" when the stock sells at or through a specific price (called the stop price). A stop order is ordinarily used to protect paper profits or limit the extent of possible loss.

straddle An investment strategy involving the purchase of a call option and a put option, each with identical features, at the same time.

"Street" name A term that applies to securities held in the name of the broker rather than in the name of the customer. Securities purchased on margin are held in street name. The customer can request street name for convenience or other reasons.

striking price The predetermined exercise price of a stock option.

technician or technical analyst One who studies all factors related to the actual supply and demand of stocks. The primary tools of a technician are stock charts and various technical indicators.

tender offer An offer by a company or a special group to purchase stock of another company. Usually the tender offer is made at a higher price than the prevailing market price.

third market The buying and selling of exchange-listed stocks in the over-the-counter market.

tout A Wall Street slang term referring to a highly biased recommendation to buy a stock.

trade date The date on which a transaction takes place. Five business days later is the settlement date.

treasury bill An obligation of the U.S. Government with a maturity date less than one year from date of issue. A treasury bill bears no interest but is sold to the investor at a discount prior to maturity.

treasury stock Issued stock which has been reacquired by the company from the stockholders. These shares may be held by the company indefinitely, reissued to the public or retired. Treasury stock receives no dividends and is not eligible to vote.

up-tick A term used to describe a transaction made at a price higher than the preceding transaction price. Also called a "plus tick."

volume The total number of shares traded, of an individual security or in the entire market, in a given period of time.

warrant A certificate giving the holder the right to purchase securities at a predetermined price within a predetermined time limit or perpetually. Warrants are issued directly by the company. In contrast, call options are written on stock already outstanding.

wash sale A fictitious and illegal purchase and sale of stock to create market activity. The term also applies to the repurchase of shares within 30 days which automatically disallows a loss for tax purposes.

when-issued The abbreviated form of "when, as and if issued" which refers to a security authorized for issuance but not yet issued.

wire house A stock brokerage firm having many branch offices linked by a communications network.

working capital or **net working capital** The excess of current assets over current liabilities.

yield The annual return on an investment (from dividends or interest) expressed as a percentage of either cost or current price.

yield to maturity The yield of a bond also taking into account the premium or discount of the bond.

Wall Street –
How it works

Introduction Nearly 400 years ago Wall
Street was an insignificant dirt path. Since
then, history has changed the dirt path into
the financial center of the Free World. Yet,
Wall Street, perhaps the most famous of all
streets, may also be the least understood.

Many people are frightened away by the
apparent complexities of investing. They
never learn of Wall Street's colorful history,
of its role in the American economy, and the
way stocks are bought and sold remains
a mystery.

Wise investing is indeed a challenge that
requires serious study, but a stock market
transaction is no more complicated than
buying or selling a car or a boat.

This chapter will provide a glimpse into
the past and a brief explanation of Wall
Street today.

Wall Street Defined Wall Street is a street, an address in New York City pointing straight from Roosevelt Drive near the East River to the old Trinity Church. But this is not the Wall Street people refer to when they ask, "How does Wall Street work?" or "What does Wall Street say?" That Wall Street is a marketplace.

Specifically, it is a marketplace where the merchants, agents and customers of finance meet to buy and sell stocks and bonds. It is composed of all the individual marketplaces and the total community of interests which maintain them and is regulated closely by the Securities and Exchange Commission (SEC).

Thus, the name Wall Street is a short, convenient reference to the exchanges where stocks are traded in a two-way auction process: the New York Stock Exchange (NYSE), the American Stock Exchange (AMEX) and the regional stock exchanges. Also included are: the nationwide network of broker/dealers known as the Over-The-Counter Market (OTC), the brokerage firms and their employees, and a variety of investors both individual and institutional.

Wall Street can also be defined with added precision according to its two major functions: to provide a primary market and a secondary market. Through the primary market corporations sell their stocks and bonds directly to the public thereby obtaining the money needed for expansion. The process of bringing a stock issue to the market for the first time is called "going public."

After a company has gone public, its shares are traded in the secondary market which provides the investor with an adequate number of bids to buy and offers to sell, as well as an opportunity to sell shares at any time. In the secondary market stock prices rise or fall according to supply and demand.

Each person using the Wall Street marketplace has one objective: to make money. The buyer is seeking to obtain an adequate investment return from a higher stock price or through dividend payments or both. The seller, on the other hand, may already have a capital gain or loss and would like to free the money for investment elsewhere. Their efforts, in total, form a fundamental economic process that creates new industries, new jobs and a higher standard of living.

Meeting under the buttonwood
tree in 1792.

A Short History The dirt path took its name from a wall of brush and mud built alongside it shortly after New York was founded as a Dutch trading post in 1609. The wall, later improved with a wooden fence, was built to keep cows in and Indians out. Although little is known about its success with cows, by 1626, Indians were certainly allowed to enter the early business community, at least long enough to sell Manhattan for $24 and some beads. The street, however, quickly became a center of commercial activity because it connected the docks serving the Hudson River trade on one end with the East River importing business at its other end.

Early merchants had many interests. They bought and sold commodities such as furs, molasses and tobacco; they traded in currencies; they insured cargos and they speculated in land. They did not, however, formally invest in stocks and bonds, for even as late as George Washington's inauguration, Wall Street had no securities exchange. In fact, this country's first stock exchange was established in Philadelphia in 1790.

In 1789, the first Congress of the United States met in Federal Hall on Wall Street, the place where George Washington had been inaugurated earlier that year as President. The first order of business was to authorize the issue of $80 million in government bonds to absorb the cost of the war. Two years later, bank stocks were added to government bonds when Alexander Hamilton, then Secretary of the Treasury, established the nation's first bank, the Bank of the United States, and offered shares to the public.

Now there were securities to trade, but still no organized market existed on Wall Street. Investors, by word of mouth, indicated their interest in any available issue through Wall Street coffee houses or by advertising in newspapers. As the list of securities grew with more bank stocks and newly formed insurance companies, a need for an organized market developed.

By early 1792, Wall Street was enjoying its first bull market. Several merchants, encouraged by the increased activity, kept a small inventory of securities on hand which would be sold over the counter like any other of their wares. Today's Over-The-Counter market got its name from this early form of trading. Business was booming. Some days as many as 100 bank shares would be traded.

Wall Street businessmen began to schedule stock and bond auctions, as they had for commodities. Soon, several leading merchants organized a central auction at 22 Wall Street where securities were traded every day at noon. Customers of the newly formed "Stock Exchange Office," or their agents, left securities with the auctioneers who received a commission for each stock or bond sold. A customer's agent, or broker, would also receive a commission for shares purchased.

With predictable ingenuity, some businessmen came to the auction only to listen. They noted the prices and, after the auction, would offer the same securities but at reduced commission rates. Even auction members traded in this after-hours market.

On March 21, 1792, concerned Wall Street leaders met at Corre's Hotel to establish an improved auction market which would also better serve their own interests. On May 17, 1792, twenty-four men signed a document in which they agreed to trade securities only among themselves, to maintain fixed commission rates and to avoid other auctions. These men are considered to be the original members of the New York Stock Exchange.

For a while, the new broker's union met under an aging buttonwood tree facing 68

Wall Street, but they soon moved indoors when the Tontine Coffee House was completed in 1793 at the northwest corner of Wall and William Streets. They prospered and moved to larger quarters in what is now 40 Wall Street. On March 8, 1817, the members adopted a formal constitution creating the New York Stock and Exchange Board. Every morning a list of all the stocks to be auctioned was read to the assembled board members who would then make bids and offers while seated. Only members were allowed to trade and the privilege to sit at the auction cost $400. To this day, a member of the NYSE is said to own a "seat," although he is never seated while trading.

Tontine Coffee House, 1793

The Board moved several times until it took space in a building located at the present NYSE site in 1863. Also that year, its present name was adopted. The building occupied by the NYSE today was completed in 1903.

Brokers not able to afford a seat on the Board or who were simply refused membership often found it difficult to make a living. In poor markets, many went bankrupt. Others drifted away to take odd-jobs elsewhere only to return for another try when business improved.

By 1850, Wall Street was throbbing with activity. Gold had been discovered in California and the country turned its attention to the West. Mining stocks and railroad shares were especially popular. Many issues, considered too speculative by the Board, were eagerly traded by non-members. Few could afford office space so they traded in the street. By the late 1870's, the corner of William and Beaver Streets filled daily with brokers shouting out orders to buy and sell. They were called "curbstone brokers" and their market was known as the Curb.

In the early 1890's, when the Curb was moved to Broad Street for more room, many brokers took offices in the nearby Mills Building. There, telephone clerks took orders and shouted them to the brokers below. But with several hundred brokers being called, more or less simultaneously, shouting soon proved futile. A system of hand signaling was developed (parts of which are still used today) to convey price and volume information to the waiting brokers. Clerks would lean out the windows of the Mills Building or balance precariously on an outside ledge working their fingers furiously. The brokers below often wore brightly-colored or otherwise distinctive clothing allowing the clerks to spot them in the crowd. Although it looked like pandemonium, the brokers knew that certain stocks were traded at specific landmarks, usually lamp posts. Action was brisk in any kind of weather.

In 1908, Emanuel S. Mendels, Jr., a leading curbstone broker, organized the Curb Market Agency which developed appropriate trading rules but had little enforcement power. In 1911, Mendels and his advisors drew up a constitution and formed the New York Curb Market Association.

One of the most colorful spectacles in American business ended on the morning of June 27, 1921. Edward McCormick, the Curb Market's chairman, led the curbstone brokers in a march up Wall Street to their newly-completed building on Trinity Place behind Trinity Church. They sang the "Star Spangled Banner" and went inside to begin their first session on the new trading floor. Inside, each trading post was marked by a lamp post which, interestingly, resembled those left behind on the street.

In 1953, the New York Curb Exchange, as it was called after 1928, adopted its present name, the American Stock Exchange.

The Primary Market The investment process begins with a primary market. Its focal point is the "investment banker," an important member of Wall Street who specializes in raising the capital business requires for long term growth. He guides a company into the public marketplace and generally helps the company in its dealings with Wall Street.

Assume, for example, that a company has enjoyed several years of business success and is now ready to expand. The company management has determined that $3 million is needed for plant expansion. An investment banker is contacted to explore financing alternatives including the possibility of going public.

Before recommending a specific method of financing, the investment banker must consider several factors such as general economic conditions, the Wall Street market environment and the company's particular circumstances including its financial condition, earnings history and business prospects. These and other factors would also be used to establish an offering price.

In this case, it is decided that a public offering of common stock would be appropriate as opposed to a form of debt obligation.

The New York Stock Exchange in session just after the Civil War and today.

The investment banker agrees to "under-write" the issue by buying all the shares for resale at a pre-established price per share. If the issue were larger, the risk could be spread by inviting other investment bankers to join in an underwriting group or "syndicate." At the time of sale, the syndicate usually invites other security dealers to join them in a selling group and together they sell the new shares to the public at a set price. Before a new issue can be sold, however, the company must comply with the full disclosure requirements of the Securities and Exchange Commission. In a registration statement filed with the SEC, the company lists the essential facts of its financial condition and operations. These facts must also be printed in a "prospectus" which members of the selling group must give to every buyer or potential buyer.

The company pays all underwriting costs allowing the buyer to purchase the stock free of any commissions or other charges. In general, this is the only time a stock price is ever fixed — when the price is temporarily supported by the investment banker. After that, the shares are traded as usual, according to supply and demand, in the secondary market.

The Secondary Market Just as a corporate treasurer works closely with an investment banker in the primary market, the investor's main contact in the secondary market is the registered representative.

This title means that this individual is "registered" with the SEC and "represents" the firm's brokers and dealers who actually execute a customer's order on the trading floor of an exchange or in the OTC market. The representative does not buy from or sell to the customer, but rather acts on the customer's behalf as an agent.

The registered representative, also known as a "stockbroker" or "account executive," and the brokerage firm are compensated by a "brokerage commission" which is charged each time a stock is bought or sold. In the OTC market, a customer may pay a "mark-up" or a "mark-down" or a commission depending on how the order is handled. A mark-up is an amount added to the purchase price while a mark-down is subtracted from the sales price by the OTC broker/dealer. The actual mark-up or mark-down must conform to National Association of Security Dealers (NASD) regulations limiting the amount which may be charged. The NASD regulates the OTC market under the supervision of the SEC.

Prior to May 1, 1975, an investor could expect to pay a predetermined minimum commission depending upon the number of shares involved and the price, for any stock listed on an exchange. This system of minimum fixed commission rates was abandoned on May 1, ending a practice which began when the first members of the NYSE agreed to charge fixed rates in 1792. At the SEC's direction, commission charges on all orders were made fully negotiable. Thus, it is now possible for an investor, who would have had no choice but to pay roughly $50 in commissions under the old schedule for 100 shares of a $25 stock, to bargain with the brokers for the lowest commission rate available.

Of course, major financial institutions, such as pension funds, banks, insurance companies and mutual funds, have the greatest bargaining power due to the large amounts of stock, often called "blocks," in each order.

In addition to varying commission rates, brokerage firms, also called "brokerage houses," differ by the types of services offered. The main office of a large NYSE member firm, for example, usually includes trading departments for exchange-listed stocks, OTC stocks, and various types of bonds; a research department where security analysts appraise the investment potential of securities; an underwriting department for new issues; a corporate finance department for investment banking, and appropriate record keeping departments for account maintenance and securities safe keeping. Other firms may offer only a few of these services and still others specialize strictly in order execution. All firms, however, must conform to extensive SEC requirements as well as additional exchange or OTC rules. Cash and securities held in custody are usually insured by the Security Investors Protection Corporation (a federal corporation), and by other insurance companies.

Finally, a brokerage firm can be differentiated on the basis of exchange memberships and by the source of their commission income. Only an exchange member is allowed to execute orders on the trading floor of an exchange. To become a member, a brokerage firm must buy a "seat," an expression which recalls the days when brokers were seated during the stock auctions. Since there is a limited number available, seats, like stocks, have their own auction market. The highest price ever paid for a NYSE seat was $515,000 in 1969. Firms not owning seats are called "non-member" firms. Their orders for exchange-listed stocks must be processed through a member firm or be executed in the so-called

"Third Market" (buying and selling exchange-listed stocks in the OTC market). A brokerage firm doing most of its commission business with individual investors is referred to as a "retail house" while a firm emphasizing institutional business by servicing mutual funds, pension funds, insurance companies and banks is called an "institutional house."

Just as brokerage firms differ, the markets are also different in terms of both listing requirements and methods of execution.

When a stock is "listed" on an exchange, it means that the stock has been accepted for trading there. The term recalls the "list" of stocks that was read to the assembled brokers at the daily auctions more than a century ago. Before its stock can be listed, the company must meet certain minimum listing requirements.

Each exchange has it own minimums. For a company to be among the nearly 1,600 listed on the NYSE, for example, it must have pretax earnings of $2.5 million, a total of 1 million shares publicly held, net tangible assets of $16 million and at least 2,000 holders of 100 share units. The NASD imposes similar, but less stringent, require-

ments before a company is accepted for quotation in the computerized National Association of Security Dealers Automatic Quotation System (abbreviated NASDAQ and pronounced "nazdak") of the OTC market. A company can be "delisted" if it falls below certain other minimum requirements.

The net effect of the various listing requirements has been to attract the oldest, largest and best known companies to the NYSE; smaller and younger companies to the AMEX and the youngest, least experienced companies to the OTC market. But there are some important exceptions. Several large, well-known companies such as Betz Laboratories, Tampax, Yellow Freight and others have not sought NYSE listing by their own choice. Today, many of the NYSE's most actively traded stocks are quoted on NASDAQ and are thus traded in the Third Market.

A company can be listed on more than one exchange. Dual listings are common on the regional exchanges where transactions in dually-traded issues are usually based on current NYSE or AMEX prices. Still, many companies listed on the regional exchanges are local or regional businesses.

There are currently 10 regional exchanges. Eight, including the three largest, the Midwest Stock Exchange, the Pacific Stock Exchange and the Philadelphia Stock Exchange, are registered with the SEC, while the remaining two are exempt because of their small size and volume. In general, the regional exchanges increase the overall liquidity of the market place.

Since 1978, the five larger regional exchanges (the Pacific, Midwest, Philadelphia, Boston and Cincinnati exchanges) have been linked by computer (I.T.S.) with the New York and American exchanges. This has led to a truly national listing for many stocks.

One major difference between the exchanges and the OTC market is the method of order execution. Trading on an exchange is accomplished by a two-way auction process while OTC trading by negotiation.

How The System Works After opening an account with a brokerage firm, similar in many ways to opening a bank account, the investor is free to buy or sell stocks through any exchange or OTC. Consider this example of a NYSE listed stock and visualize how the important forces of supply and demand influence the stock price.

A shopkeeper in Atlanta, Georgia goes to his local broker, a member firm, and gives his registered representative a "market order" to buy 100 shares (the standard unit of trading commonly called a "round lot") of the XYZ Company. A market order is an order to be executed as soon as possible at the best price available. At about the same time, a teacher in Denver, Colorado places a market order with her local broker, also a member firm, to sell 100 shares of XYZ stock. The orders are quickly sent to the trading departments of the respective firms and then transmitted directly to the floor of the NYSE. The firms' "floor brokers," employees located on the trading floor, receive the orders from one of several tele-type machines serving the trading area.

Once the floor brokers have the orders, they proceed to the "trading post" where XYZ is bought and sold. Each listed stock is traded at one of several specific locations or posts and each listed stock has a "specialist" assigned to it. The specialist's primary function is "to insure a fair and orderly market" in each assigned stock by buying and selling for his own account in the absence of other competing bids and offers.

At the post, the brokers enter the "crowd" a group of two or more brokers who also have orders for XYZ. "How's XYZ?" asks the broker representing the Atlanta shopkeeper. "Thirty and three-eighths to three-quarters," someone — usually the specialist — responds. This is the current "bid and asked" quotation. This means that 30 3/8 is the best bid, the most anyone in the crowd is then willing to pay; and 30 3/4 is the best offer, the lowest price at which anyone will sell. The difference between the two is called the "spread."

The shopkeeper's broker will try to get a better price than the offer by saying "30 1/2 for one hundred," but if there is no response, the broker will raise the bid in increments of 1/8 of a dollar, the minimum unit of change for most stocks. Perhaps at 30 5/8, the teacher's broker hollers "sold" feeling that it is the best price he can expect at that time. The transaction has been completed. The customers are notified by their registered representatives often within minutes after the order was first sent to the floor. The company's stock symbol, usually an abbreviaton of the name, and the execution price of the trade are both printed immediately on the consolidated ticker tape which is displayed electronically in brokerage offices throughout the country.

If there had been no offers to sell stock when the floor broker representing the Atlanta customer arrived at the post, the specialist would have filled the order himself by selling stock from his own account. Similarly, if the broker had a sell order, the specialist would have bought the stock for his own account. The specialist's bid and asked quotation reflects the orders in his "specialist's book," a notebook containing special types of customer orders for each assigned stock. Orders in the specialist's book cannot be executed immediately because they are "away from the market," that is, they are above or below the price at which that stock is currently being traded. The specialist, or his specialist firm, must always have enough capital on hand to buy 2,000 shares of any stock he has been assigned. In discharging his responsibility to preserve a fair and orderly market, the specialist attempts to keep the spread narrow and minimize any sharp price fluctuation either up or down.

When the specialist trades for his own account, he is said to be acting as a "dealer," much like the dealers in the OTC market. A dealer acts as a principal in a transaction buying from and selling stock to a customer. A broker, on the other hand, only represents a customer as a middleman or agent.

The specialist also acts as a dealer if an investor wants to buy or sell from 1 to 99 shares, called an "odd-lot." On the NYSE, an odd-lot order is processed by computer and is automatically executed at the next round-lot price struck at the post. The specialist receives periodic reports telling him how many odd-lot shares have been added to or subtracted from his inventory. For this service, the specialist usually charges the customer an additional 1/8 point (12 1/2 cents) per share, traditionally called the "odd-lot differential."

Prior to January, 1976, odd-lot orders had been filled by Carlisle, Decoppet & Company, a highly specialized brokerage firm which had been the solely enfranchised odd-lot dealer on the NYSE. The firm withdrew from the odd-lot business in January. A principal reason was that its largest customer, Merrill, Lynch, Pierce, Fenner, & Smith, Inc., began to fill odd-lot orders for customers through its own internal dealer market. The Merrill, Lynch program was designed to reduce a customer's commission costs by eliminating the differential.

If the Atlanta shopkeeper wanted to buy 100 shares of an OTC stock rather than an exchange-listed stock, the order would have been sent to the firm's OTC trading desk.

The old Edison "dome" stock ticker is now a relic of the past.

The individuals at the desk are referred to as "broker/dealers" because they can act in either capacity depending on the circumstances.

The shopkeeper's order may be filled directly from the firm's inventory if the broker/dealer "makes a market" in the stock. In this case, the broker/dealer acts as a principal, or, in other words, as a dealer. As a market maker, the dealer maintains an inventory of the stock, must be prepared to buy or sell at least 100 shares at any time and must announce bid and asked prices continuously. The OTC trading department, through the registered representative, quotes a single "net price" to the customer which includes the dealer's mark-up. The customer is free to negotiate for a lower price. The order is completed as soon as the customer and the dealer agree.

If the broker/dealer does not make a market in the stock and the stock is quoted in the NASDAQ System, the broker/dealer interrogates the system's computer by typing the trading symbol of the stock onto a keyboard attached to an electronic display screen. The names and bid and asked quotations of all market makers in that stock instantly appear on the screen.

The broker/dealer then calls the market maker offering the best quote, negotiates a price and buys the stock for the customer. The broker/dealer has acted as a broker or agent and charges the customer a commission.

If the stock is not among the nearly 4,000 stocks currently being quoted on NASDAQ, the broker/dealer will have to negotiate a price with one of the market makers listed in the "pink sheets," a daily list of all OTC market makers and their quotes published by the National Quotation Service. The process takes longer but is otherwise identical to a NASDAQ System trade.

The OTC Market is the oldest and largest securities market in the country. Although it does not meet in any one central place, OTC broker/dealers are connected by the computer of the NASDAQ System and by telephone. Traded in the OTC market are almost all federal, state, municipal and corporate bonds, almost all new issues, most mutual funds, several foreign stocks and nearly 30,000 domestic stocks. The aggregate dollar volume of the OTC market greatly exceeds the dollar volume executed on all stock exchanges combined.

Who Buys Stock? Common stock ownership is broadly separated into two categories: individual and institutional.

In recent years, investor surveys have placed the number of individual shareholders between 25 and 30 million. Although stockholder characteristics vary widely, one survey found that the average shareowner had a median age of 53, an annual household income of $19,000, a stock portfolio valued at $10,050, a college education and a professional or technical job. In addition, more women owned stock than did men.

The individual shareholder once owned the largest portion of all stock outstanding. During the past decade, however, institutional investors have steadily replaced individuals as the most important factor in the stock market. Today, institutional investors hold roughly one-third of the $961 billion total market value for all NYSE listed stocks. If the holdings of foreign institutions, private funds, and certain other funds were included, statisticians estimate that total institutional holdings could even represent one-half of all NYSE stocks. The largest institutional investors, ranked by the market value of their holdings, have

been: non-insured pension funds, investment companies, non-profit institutions, insurance companies, common trust funds, and mutual savings banks.

The table on the next page presents trading activity of the major markets in greater detail. The actual number of shares traded was considerably higher because the figures do not include Over-The-Counter stocks outside the NASDAQ System.

Approximate 1982 Share Volume

Market	Shares Traded	Percent of Total Shares Traded
New York Stock Exchange	13,750,000,000	59%
NASDAQ	7,500,000,000	32%
American Stock Exchange	1,100,000,000	5%
Other Exchanges	1,000,000,000	4%
Total	**23,350,000,000**	**100%**

Source: Author estimates

The Future In the Securities Acts Amendments of 1975, Congress authorized the SEC to facilitate the establishment of a centralized National Market System.

The National Market System is expected by many to modernize and improve the investment process in keeping with the dramatic technological changes of the past 40 years, to make it more efficient by eliminating needless duplication and to centralize all buying and selling interest. Computer programs are already being tested to consolidate trading activity on the various exchanges. By uniting separate markets, these programs attempt to expose each order to the best bid and asked prices no matter where they occur.

Change, however, comes slowly to the nation's financial markets. Pieces of the System are being placed one at a time. The NYSE and the AMEX, for example, now display consolidated tapes which report transactions in their dually or multiply-listed issues occurring on the regional exchanges or Over-The-Counter.

The process of change that began in the 1970's is expected to accelerate in the current decade. Eventually, Wall Street may once again hear the words spoken in 1921 by Edward McCormick. Just before the curbstone brokers went inside for the first time, he said: "The die is cast. The old order is gone forever."

Understanding your company

Introduction The company whose stock
performs best in the long run — ten or
twenty years — usually has a superior
record of earnings, dividends and improved
financial condition. An individual investor
will find it easier to identify such a company once the rudiments of security analysis are mastered. This chapter will show
how to read corporate financial statements
and will highlight the most important
analytical concepts used by successful
long term investors.

Getting to Know the Company "What is this company's business?" is the first question an investor should ask. The president of a diversified company might answer, "Oh, we're in business to make money" or "We make motorbikes, golf clubs, tennis balls and football helmets." Yet, like a ship, a company must have a charted course to follow. An answer such as: "We manufacture and sell quality sporting goods for the leisure-time market" would indicate that the company has a corporate strategy. Before anything else, an investor should know the corporate purpose and have confidence that management also knows.

There are various ways an investor can become acquainted with a company. First, and most important, is through the company's literature . . . past annual reports, quarterly statements, management speeches and press releases. This information can be obtained free of charge by writing to the secretary of the corporation. The company's mailing address is available at any brokerage office or in research books in the public library.

Research reports written by securities analysts of brokerage firms provide another way to learn about a company. The typical brokerage report ordinarily deals with an analysis of current earnings prospects, but rarely provides the necessary insight into the industry, competition, or the management. However, these reports help investors better understand current operations and problems. The investor should read the reports, extract factual information, and avoid unsubstantiated assumptions. The investment decision should be made by the investor alone after studying all the information available.

A third way to learn about a company is by attending its annual meeting. Depending upon company policy, it is sometimes possible to attend without being a stockholder or a stockholder "guest." A call or letter to the company's secretary will answer the question.

Annual meetings can be interesting because the corporate executives want to make a favorable impression. At the same time, investors are trying to look beneath smooth or clumsy presentations for any indication of management talent or weakness. Company presentations become increasingly valuable as the investor gains experience through exposure to different companies.

The meeting is usually held at or near the corporate headquarters, although many large, widely-held companies accommodate stockholders by holding the meeting in a different city each year. In most cases, it is scheduled for the same day every year according to the company's by-laws. The date, time and location of the annual meeting normally can be found on the inside cover of the annual report or in a variety of other places including the public library.

One major order of business at the annual meeting is the election of the company's directors by the stockholders. A few weeks prior to the meeting the company will mail a "proxy statement" to each stockholder. The stockholder reviews the proxy material, decides how to vote on the election and other proposals, fills out the proxy and returns it to the company to be counted like any other election ballot.

The business portion of the meeting usually takes a few minutes but can continue for an hour or so including the stockholders' question and answer period. Sometimes the annual meeting also includes a tour of the company's offices or factories. In fact, several companies such as the Polaroid Corporation, General Motors and others are well known for holding stimulating annual meetings. If it is possible to attend, an investor will find a well-organized annual meeting an interesting and worthwhile experience.

*Texas Instruments
Introduces Portable
Computer Terminal*

Financial Statements The annual report, usually published a few months after the company's fiscal year ends, is the best place to begin the analysis of a company. The typical report contains the President's Letter to Stockholders which outlines the events of the past year and the present status of the corporation. The body of the report explains the company's business operations in greater detail. Located in the back is the financial section, the most revealing part of any annual report. This section contains three important financial statements:

- The Income Statement
- The Balance Sheet
- The Source & Application of Funds Statement

The *Income Statement* presents the company's business results for the year. It shows, in dollar terms, the company's sales, costs and earnings (profits) over the past twelve months compared with the preceding twelve month period.

The *Balance Sheet* presents the company's financial condition at the end of the year by listing: (1) What the company *owns* (assets such as cash, inventory, factories, equipment, etc.); (2) What the company *owes* (liabilities such as short term bank borrowings and long term debt) and (3) The "stockholders' equity" which is the difference between the assets and liabilities. On every balance sheet the total assets figure is always equal to the total liabilities figure plus the stockholders' equity figure.

The *Source and Application of Funds Statement* is best described as a bridge between the Income Statement and the Balance Sheet. It explains exactly how the company's financial position changed during the year. In short, the Source and Application of Funds Statement outlines how the company financed its growth during the year (i.e., the "source," where the money came from, and the "applications," where the money went).

All three statements are accompanied by a series of footnotes which explain the figures in greater detail. Sometimes these footnotes contain significant information and are worth reading. In addition, there is a table showing several years of financial history. This table generally includes income data, balance sheet data and supplementary statistics that can further help an investor understand the company and its background.

Finally, the financial section contains a report submitted by an independent accounting expert indicating that the statements were prepared in accordance with generally accepted accounting principles and that the financial statements present, fairly and on a consistent basis, the financial position of the company for the years noted. The investor should read it to check for any "qualifications" the auditors considered important.

To better understand the example to follow, an investor should be familiar with several terms...

On the Income Statement

The term *Sales* is used to describe the total dollar amount received for the products sold to customers during the period. *Cost of Products Sold,* or sometimes called

Cost of Sales, represents the cost of manufacturing these products. These costs include raw materials, wages, salaries, fuel and other direct production costs. The difference between the company's sales and cost of sales is called "gross profit." *Selling, General and Administrative Expenses* include officers' salaries, salesmen's commissions, advertising spending, research and development expenses and other general expenses. The term *Depreciation* is often used to describe the gradual decline in the value of assets such as buildings and equipment. Depreciation is not a cash outlay. Nevertheless, it is another cost of operating the business due to the reduction in service life of the property. These assets are typically in use for more than a year and, therefore, an estimated portion of their original cost is recognized as they are "used up." The *operating profit* is calculated by deducting cost of sales, SG&A expenses and depreciation from the sales figure.

Once all costs and expenses are deducted from all revenues, the profit that a company achieves before paying taxes (federal, state, local and foreign) is called *Profit Before Taxes.* The profit that a company earns after deducting taxes is referred to as *Net Earnings.*

*McDonald's Is Buying
80-Acre Expansion Site*

On the Balance Sheet

The Balance Sheet is divided into three major parts: *Assets* or what the company owns, *Liabilities* or what the company owes, and the difference between them, known as *Stockholders' Equity.* The company's assets and liabilities can be either "current" or "long term." Current refers to any time within twelve months from the date of the balance sheet, whereas long term refers to any time period beyond twelve months. *Current Assets* are assets that are expected to be converted to cash within twelve months. *Current Liabilities* are obligations that will be paid within twelve months.

Among the important items included in current assets besides cash and securities are *Accounts Receivable* (money owed to the company primarily by customers) and *Inventories* (raw materials, work in process, supplies and finished products ready to be sold).

Current liabilities usually include an *Accounts Payable* figure which represents money the company owes to raw material suppliers and others in the normal course of business. A *Notes Payable* figure in the current liability section indicates the company is obligated to pay a debt, often to a bank or a supplier, within twelve months.

One important term used frequently is "working capital" which is simply the excess of current assets over current liabilities. In the example to follow, the working capital of the XYZ Company is $630 ($946 current assets less $316 current liabilities). Sometimes current liabilities exceed current assets, although this rarely happens with good companies. When this does occur, it is said that the company has "negative working capital."

Long Term Debt is debt the company will have to repay sometime beyond twelve months from the date of the balance sheet. The footnotes of the annual report explain in greater detail the types of obligations and exactly when the debt is due for repayment. The company's long term debt could be in the form of bank debt, mortgage bonds, debenture bonds (issued solely on the credit of the company rather than secured by property) or other types of obligations.

Stockholders' Equity, sometimes called Net Worth, represents the stockholders' interest in the company and is defined as total assets less total liabilities. Included in the stockholders' equity figure would be the amount of money that has been invested directly into the company and all earnings reinvested back into the business up to the date of the balance sheet.

When a stockholder calculates the amount of equity behind each share, the result is called "book value." This figure is determined by dividing the amount of stockholders' equity by the number of shares outstanding.

In addition to common stock, many companies have preferred stock outstanding. As the name implies, these shares have preference over common stock in the payment of dividends and in the event of corporate liquidation. If preferred stock is outstanding, any amount to which preferred shareholders are entitled must first be deducted from total stockholders' equity before calculating book value of the common.

Frequently an investor will see the term "par value" applied to common stock. Par value is an arbitrary amount put on the certificate having no relation to the market price of the stock or its liquidation value. The term is used principally for bookkeeping purposes. Due to the confusion surrounding the term, many companies simply place an arbitrary stated value on the stock and call it "no-par value stock."

The Basics of Analysis How the three financial statements are constructed, how they relate to one another and the fundamental story they tell can be seen in the example of the hypothetical, well-managed XYZ Company appearing on the next page.

The most effective means of analyzing a company is to study its record over the past few years and to compare it to other well-managed companies, preferably of the same industry or having the same financial characteristics. Companies and industries are very different. A retailer will differ from a pharmaceutical company or an airline. An electric utility will differ from a computer manufacturer or a fast food company. *However, each company and its management has one thing in common with every other company: An obligation to achieve the best possible investment return for the owners of the business (the stockholders).*

When one individual buys a share of stock from another individual he is acquiring a share of ownership in the company and part ownership in the company's equity. This equity, belonging to the stockholders, is entrusted to the management. Management has an obligation to invest this money wisely taking into consideration the company's business opportunities, its expertise and the degree of risk the stockholders are willing to assume.

52

XYZ Company Income Statement For the Year Ended December 31		XYZ C Balance Sheet	
REVENUES		**ASSETS**	
		Current Assets	
Sales to Customers	$2,225	Cash	$ 38
Interest Income	12	Marketable Securities	200
Royalty and Other Income	15	Accounts Receivable	288
Total Revenues	2,252	Inventories	397
		Other Current Assets	23
COSTS AND EXPENSES		Total Current Assets	946
Cost of Products Sold	1,100		
Selling, General and			
Administrative Expenses	755	**Long Term Assets**	
Depreciation	69	Property, Plant and	
Other Expenses	18	Equipment	528
TOTAL COSTS		Other Assets	77
AND EXPENSES	1,942	Total Long Term Assets	605
		TOTAL ASSETS	**$1,551**
PROFIT BEFORE TAXES	310		
Less:			
Federal, State and			
Foreign Taxes	126		
NET EARNINGS	**$184**		

Return on Equity

Net earnings divided by
stockholders' equity

pany **December 31**	**XYZ Company** **Source and Application** **of Funds Statement**

LIABILITIES

Current Liabilities		
Accounts Payable	$ 99	
Loans and Notes Payable	88	
Other Current Liabilities	129	
Total Current Liabilities		316
Long Term Debt		85

STOCKHOLDERS' EQUITY

Common Stock	145	
Retained Earnings	1,005	
Total Stockholders' Equity		1,150
TOTAL LIABILITIES & EQUITY		**$1,551**

SOURCE OF FUNDS

Net Earnings	$184	
Depreciation of Property	69	
Other Sources	7	
Provided by Operations		260
Increase in Long Term Debt	13	
Proceeds from Employee's Stock Options	4	
Proceeds from the Sale of Property	3	
Provided by Outside Sources		20
TOTAL		**280**

APPLICATION OF FUNDS

Additions to Property, Plant and Equipment	$136	
Cash Dividends Paid	49	
Decrease in Long Term Debt	10	
Other Applications	10	
TOTAL		**205**
INCREASE IN WORKING CAPITAL		**$ 75**

Retention Rate

Net earnings less
dividends divided by
net earnings

54

One of the most important calculations in security analysis is figuring the company's "return on equity." This ratio indicates the rate of investment return the company's executives have been able to achieve on the equity entrusted to them. A return of much less than 10% is generally regarded as unsatisfactory.

Using the example of the XYZ Company, the return on equity is calculated by dividing the net earnings figure ($184 located on the income statement) by the stockholders' equity figure ($1,150 located on the balance sheet). The return on equity of the XYZ Company is, therefore, 16%. To be more precise, it is preferable when calculating return on equity to use the *average* equity over the past year since the company's $184 income was earned over the past twelve months whereas the equity figure on the balance sheet is a year-end figure. Average equity is found by averaging the year-beginning and year-ending stockholders' equity figures. Nevertheless, the idea is the same.

Another important calculation is the "retention rate" or, in other words, the percent of net earnings reinvested back into the business rather than being paid out as dividends. The retention rate is calculated from the Source and Applications of Funds Statement by dividing the amount of net earnings reinvested back into the business (net earnings less dividends) by the net earnings figure. Last year the retention rate of the XYZ Company, for example, was 73% or $184 less $49 divided by $184.

Of course, the retention rate can also be calculated in the same manner by using the earnings per share and dividend per share figures.

A company that grows entirely by reinvesting its earnings back into the business is said to be self-financing. Generally speaking, the most successful companies today are self-financing, which can be particularly important during inflationary times.

Both the "return on equity" and the "retention rate" calculations are very important to an analyst because they provide a clue to the company's internal growth rate potential for earnings (analysts refer to this growth potential as the "reinvestment rate"). A company can only grow either: (1) By plowing earnings back into the business, or (2) By obtaining new debt or equity capital from outside the company.

The reinvestment rate is simply the product of the return on equity and the retention rate as shown in the formula above.

Reinvestment Rate = Return on Equity X Retention Rate

The internal growth potential of the XYZ Company is, therefore:

Reinvestment Rate		Return on Equity	X	Retention Rate
↓	=	↓	X	↓
11.7%	=	16%	X	73%

It can be seen from the formula that a company can improve its reinvestment rate by either increasing its return on equity or expanding its retention rate or a combination of both.

The retention rate is influenced directly by the dividend policy of the company and can be adjusted at will by management, while improving the return on equity is a more complex task as illustrated later.

Any substantial enhancement or deterioration of a company's reinvestment rate can influence the market performance of its stock. Consequently, every serious investor should understand this formula and recognize its limitations.

At certain times the formula can be misleading. For instance, a low-quality company can achieve a high return on equity by simply showing a profit with a small amount of equity (perhaps the result of many unprofitable years). For this reason, it is also advisable to calculate the company's "return on total assets" (net income divided by the total assets). When *both* return on equity and return on assets are high, the reinvestment rate can be used with greater confidence.

In addition to the reinvestment rate formula, there are many other statistical calculations that can be applied when analyzing companies. Here are a few using the figures of the XYZ Company:

Operating Profit Margin
(Income Statement)

$$\text{Operating Profit Margin} = \frac{\text{Operating Profits}}{\text{Sales}}$$

$$13.5\% = \frac{\$301}{\$2,225}$$

This calculation tells an investor how profitable the company's products are to manufacture and sell. An operating profit margin of less than 8% is usually regarded to be unsatisfactory for manufacturing companies.

Pretax Profit Margin (Income Statement)

$$\text{Pretax Profit Margin} = \frac{\text{Profit Before Taxes}}{\text{Total Revenues}}$$

$$13.8\% = \frac{\$310}{\$2,252}$$

The pretax profit margin, or pretax margin as it is often called, shows an investor how profitable the company's operations have been, taking into account all sources of income and all costs, before paying income taxes.

Tax Rate (Income Statement)

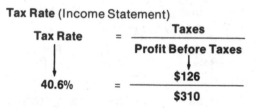

$$\text{Tax Rate} = \frac{\text{Taxes}}{\text{Profit Before Taxes}}$$

$$40.6\% = \frac{\$126}{\$310}$$

The tax rate calculation shows the percent of profits paid to federal, state, local and foreign governments—usually in the form of income taxes. Most often a company's tax rate will be in the 47-52% range. However, the tax rate could be lower for several reasons. Perhaps the company has a plant in a foreign country with a low tax rate or perhaps the company has taken advantage of various tax credits (allowances for unprofitable operations in previous years or incentives established by the government for one reason or another).

Net Profit Margin (Income Statement)

$$\text{Net Profit Margin} = \frac{\text{Net Earnings}}{\text{Total Revenues}}$$

$$8.2\% = \frac{\$184}{\$2,252}$$

The net profit margin measures a company's profitability after all costs, expenses and taxes have been paid. For U.S. companies, 5-6% has been typical in recent years.

Current Ratio (Balance Sheet)

$$\text{Current Ratio} = \frac{\text{Current Assets}}{\text{Current Liabilities}}$$

$$3.0 = \frac{\$946}{\$316}$$

The current ratio is one measure of financial strength. A ratio of 2.0 or higher is desirable although a somewhat lower current ratio might still be considered healthy if current assets are mostly cash or the business is cash-oriented. A ratio of more than 5.0 could indicate that business volume is not meeting expectations or that the company's assets are not being employed to their best advantage.

Another current relationship is the ratio of cash and equivalents (e.g., marketable securities) to current liabilities. This is sometimes called the "acid test ratio." The acid test ratio of the XYZ Company last year was 75% ($38 + $200 divided by $316).

Captial Structure (Balance Sheet)

The capital structure, frequently called "capitalization," is the total money invested in a company, including both bonds (long term debt) and equity. The capital structure of the XYZ Company, for example, appears as follows:

Long Term Debt	$ 85	7%
Stockholders' Equity	1,150	93%
Total Capitalization	$1,235	100%

The XYZ Company is conservatively managed judging by the low amount of debt within the total capital structure. This is a desirable quality since it permits management greater flexibility during difficult economic times. Unless the company is a utility or in a finance-oriented business, the general rule is: the greater the proportion of debt, the greater the risk to the stockholder.

Cash Flow (Source and Applications of Funds Statement)

$$\text{Cash Flow} = \text{Net Income} + \text{Depreciation}$$

$$\$253 = \$184 + \$69$$

Cash flow can be helpful in the analysis of profit trends and in measuring a company's ability to finance its construction programs. It is especially meaningful when comparing companies because not all depreciate their assets at the same rate. It can be seen from the Source and Applications Statement how important the cash flow items of net income and depreciation can be. Depreciation is regarded as a source of capital because it is a non-cash expense on the Income Statement.

The earnings per share figure is probably more closely monitored by the financial community than any other company statistic. It is calculated simply by dividing net earnings by the number of shares outstanding.

Using the XYZ Company as an example, if net earnings last year happened to be $184 million and the company had 40 million shares outstanding, the earnings per share of the XYZ Company would be $4.60 per share. Sometimes the number of shares outstanding changes during the year. When this occurs, the earnings per share calculation is usually based on the average number of shares outstanding during the year rather than the number of shares outstanding at year end.

The earnings per share figure can be calculated another way, which, once more, illustrates a relationship between the company's financial statements:

Earnings Per Share	=	Return on Equity	X	Book Value Per Share
$4.60	=	16%	X	$28.75

Other Analytical Concepts The importance of management attaining a high profit return on the stockholders' investment cannot be over-emphasized. As additional money is invested into the business (either as new capital or reinvested earnings) sales should increase. Sales growth is important, but has little meaning if each incremental sales dollar does not produce the profit to justify the new investment. For these reasons, an investor should watch for trends in sales, profit margins and return on equity.

A sales increase or decline can occur in any or all of these three ways: (1) An increase or decline in the absolute number of units sold; (2) Higher or lower selling prices of each unit; (3) If a company's products are sold overseas, an increase or decline in the values of currencies between countries. These factors should be recognized when sales growth is being monitored.

Another effective method of measuring a company's sales progress is watching for a trend in "equity turnover" (sales divided by average stockholders' equity). The level of equity turnover often reflects the type of business in which the

Industry	ROE%				
Aerospace	16%	Conglomerates	12%	Office Equipment	17%
Airlines	NIL	Drugs	19%	Paper	16%
Automotive	15%	Electronics	15%	Railroads	8%
Banks	11%	Food Processing	16%	Retailing (non food)	13%
Beverages	16%	Food Retailing	13%	Steels	8%
Broadcasting	20%	Machinery	14%	Textiles & Apparel	13%
Building Materials	12%	Metals & Mining	7%	Tire & Rubber	9%
Chemicals	15%	Natural Resources	14%	Utilities	11%

company is engaged. As a general rule, companies with high profit margins usually have a low equity turnover while companies with low profitability usually have a high equity turnover. A trend, either up or down, could be important.

Sales growth loses significance if it is not translated into earnings "at the bottom line." Net earnings, of course, is the primary means of increasing stockholders' equity. When sales advance more rapidly than costs and expenses, profit margins expand and vice versa. As explained earlier, profit margins can be analyzed many ways — by using the operating profit margin, the pretax profit margin and the net profit margin.

A company can improve its return on equity by either increasing its equity turnover or its profitability or both as the following formula demonstrates, again using the XYZ Company as an example:

For the XYZ Company to improve its return on equity to, say, 18% from 16%, management would either have to achieve a net profit margin closer to 9% or increase the equity turnover to more than 2.2 or a combination of both.

Return on equity is not the same for every industry as the table above illustrates. At mid-year 1976, the average return on equity for the major industries in the U.S. was just over 13%.

Some industries are regarded as "growth" industries while others are referred to as "basic" industries. Generally speaking, growth industries have consistently superior profitability and usually allocate less money to build new plant (that is, they are less capital-intensive). An investor should realize, too, that within each industry some companies are more profitable than others.

Return on Equity		Net Profit Margin	X	Equity Turnover
↓		↓		↓
16%	=	8%	X	2.0

Conclusion Statistical analytical concepts are important, to be sure, but there are many questions still to be answered in the selection process. Among them:

- What is the company's primary business?

- Is the company a leader in its industry?

- Will there be good demand for the company's products or services in the years ahead?

- Who are the principal competitors and can the company compete?

- What are the strengths and weaknesses of management?

- What are management's goals and objectives?

- Does management recognize its responsibilities to the stockholders of the company?

Once the statistical methods outlined in this chapter become almost routine, the investor should find security analysis an enjoyable challenge. Moreover, it is especially gratifying to know you understand your company.

Reading
the financial
pages

Introduction Reading the financial section of a newspaper is much like watching a football game. Neither one makes much sense unless you know the rules, understand the objectives and can identify a few players.

Some readers may even quit before they begin, discouraged by what appear to be endless columns of meaningless numbers and equally unintelligible graphs.

But the financial pages, although they seem confusing, are not difficult to understand.

This chapter will help explain why many people open directly to the business section before any other and why they consider reading the financial pages part of the excitement of Wall Street.

Allied Corp	General Electric	Owens-Illinois
Aluminum Co	General Foods	Procter & Gamb
Amer Brands	General Motors	Sears Roebuck
Amer Can	Goodyear	Std Oil of Calif
Amer Express	Inco	Texaco
Amer Tel & Tel	IBM	Union Carbide
Bethlehem Steel	Inter Harvester	United Technologies
DuPont	Inter Paper	US Steel
Eastman Kodak	Merck	Westinghouse El
Exxon	Minnesota M&M	Woolworth

The Dow Jones Averages The Dow Jones Averages are, by far, the most popular indicators of overall, day-to-day stock market direction. Charles H. Dow, one of the founders of Dow Jones Company and first editor of the *Wall Street Journal,* is credited with the original 1884 calculations of what are still, to this day, the most widely followed stock market averages in the world. It was his intention to express the general level and trend of the stock market by using the average prices of a few representative stocks.

In 1896, there were two Dow Jones averages. Most important at the time was the Dow Jones Railroad Average comprised of 20 rail stocks. The other average, containing 12 stocks representing all other types of businesses, was called the Dow Jones Industrial Average (DJIA). In 1916 the Industrial Average was increased to 20 stocks. Twelve years later, in 1928, it was increased to 30 stocks, the same number used today.

A third index, the Dow Jones Utility Average, was established as a 20 stock average in 1929 — later reduced to 15 stocks, as it is today. The three averages, the *30 Industrials,* now regarded as the most important; the *20 Transportations,* revised and renamed to include airlines and truck-

ing stocks; and, the *15 Utilities* together comprise the fourth index, the 65 Dow Jones Composite.

Over the years, the widely-followed Dow Jones Industrial Average has changed considerably with many substitutions. Fewer than twenty of the thirty stocks in 1928 remain and only General Electric and American Brands (formerly American Tobacco) of the present Industrial average were included in Dow's original computation. The 30 stocks currently used to compute the Dow Jones Industrial Average appear above.

The Industrial Average is simply an average of the prices of these thirty stocks. However, when one of the thirty companies declares a stock split or a stock dividend (explained on page 74) the divisor has to be decreased accordingly to maintain comparability. Today the divisor, instead of being 30, is under 1.50.

With the passing of time, the level of the Industrial Average has increased reflecting the growth of the companies in the average. From 1915 to about 1925, the DJIA fluctuated around the 100 mark. During the economic boom of the late 1920's, the index rose culminating with the 1929 peak of 386. The sharp stock market plunge in late 1929 and the steep

The Dow Jones Industrial Average, comprised of thirty major companies, is recognized and quoted worldwide.

decline of the Great Depression took the DJIA back to below 100 in the early 1930's. The venerable index remained in the 100-200 range throughout the late 1930's and during the decade of the 1940's. The Dow Jones Industrials advanced in the post-World War II bull market from under 200 to above 700. Following a sharp setback in 1962, the index continued to climb to the "magic 1000" mark, reached for the first time in early 1966. It is interesting to note that IBM was replaced by American Telephone within the Dow Jones Industrial Average in 1939. Had this substitution not been made, the DJIA would have crossed the 1000 mark four years before it did.

The 1966-80 period brought several sharp swings in the stock market taking the Dow Industrials on a roller coaster ride few investors will ever forget. After reaching 1000 in early 1966, the index declined in the following months to 736. By late 1968, it was again approaching 1000 only to turn down and touch a low of 627 less than two years later. Climbing back again, the Industrials reached a peak of 1067 in early 1973 which preceded the sharpest bear market in forty years. When the Dow Jones Industrials touched 570 on a gloomy day in late 1974, the 1000 mark seemed more distant than ever before. However, once again the Dow Industrials crossed 1000 in early 1976.

Once the Dow Jones Industrial Average is calculated, the result is expressed in terms of "points" rather than "dollars." When a news commentator announces: "the market was up 7 points today to close at 985," what is really being said is: "the Dow Jones 30 Industrial stocks averaged 985 when calculated at 4 pm today (the end of the NYSE trading session), which is an increase of 7 points from the 978 calculation at the close of the session yesterday."

The DJIA is frequently criticized because a higher-priced stock such as Exxon tends to have a greater influence on the index than a lower-priced stock such as Inco . In addition, some people would prefer a broader list than just 30 or 65 stocks. As a result, other market averages are also used. One such average is the Standard & Poor's 500 Index which was first calculated in 1957. Weighted according to the market value of each security in it, the S & P 500 accounts for about 85% of the dollar market value of all stocks listed on the New York Stock Exchange. Another closely followed market average, the New York Stock Exchange Index, was initiated in 1966. It includes all listed stocks on the Big Board and, like the Dow Jones Averages and S & P 500, is calculated by computer several times each day.

The Dow Jones Industrial Average is an important benchmark for investors in more than one way. Not only does it provide a means of indicating overall direction of stock prices, but the index can also be used as a guide to relative values. The index has its own earnings and dividend which are averages of the earnings and dividends of the component companies. These statistics are readily available and can be used by investors as a basis for comparison with individual stocks. The same calculations are also available for the other Dow averages as well as the Standard & Poor's averages.

The Stock Tables Just as a minute is divided into sixty seconds, a foot into twelve inches or a gallon into four quarts, Wall Street divides a stock dollar into fractions of eight or, as they say, "eighths of a point." Each eighth of a dollar has a value of 12½ cents. A share of stock priced, for example, between $30 and $31 could be either 30-1/8, 30-1/4, 30-3/8, 30-1/2, 30-5/8, 30-3/4 or 30-7/8 which is another way of saying $30.125, $30.25, $30.375, $30.50, $30.625, $30.75 or $30.875.

An individual can buy one share or many shares although the broker's commission charge is proportionately lower when a greater number of shares is bought or sold. An investor who purchases 100 shares of stock at 28-5/8 would, in effect, be investing $2862.50 before being charged a brokerage commission of about $40-50 for executing the order. If this company's stock were listed on the New York Stock Exchange, this transaction or "trade" would appear next to the company's name on the NYSE table for that day. If the stock were listed on the American Stock Exchange or traded Over-the-Counter (not listed on an exchange), the transaction would be recorded in the appropriate table located elsewhere in the business section.

-1976- High	Low	Stocks	Div.	P-E Ratio	Sales 100s	High	Low	Close	Net Chg.
26⅝	18⅛	MidlRo	1.40	7	76	26	25⅝	25⅞ −	½
29½	22¾	MilesLb	1.28	9	17	25⅞	25⅜	25⅝ +	½
17⅝	9⅝	MiltBrad	.44	9	48	15¼	14⅞	15¼ +	¼
65⅛	52⅛	MinMM	1.45	23	725	56⅜	55½	56¼ +	½
20⅝	18¼	MinnPL	1.66	7	15	19¾	19½	19¾	
15¼	11⅞	MirroAl	.96	9	2	13⅜	13¼	13¼	
12¾	8	MissnEq	.28	9	72	12⅛	11⅝	12⅛ +	⅜
37⅛	22⅝	MPacC	1.40	6	527	34	33½	34 +	½

Each line of the daily stock table tells a different story. As an example, assume a long term stockholder of the Minnesota Mining & Manufacturing Company (the manufacturer of "Scotch" tape, 3M sandpaper and many other products) is reading a copy of today's *Wall Street Journal* or any other large daily newspaper. The company's stock is listed on the New York Stock Exchange and can be found alphabetically in the "M" section of the stock table with the heading "NYSE — Composite Transactions." The company's bonds are also traded on the New York Exchange and the bond transactions of the day can be found in the bond tables on another page. However, since the shareholder has been watching 3M stock for many years, its exact location in the stock table can be found very quickly. Today's paper reports the transactions that occurred yesterday as illustrated above.

The two columns to the left of the company's name show the price range of the stock over the preceding fifty-two weeks. Earlier in the year the stock traded as high as 65-1/8 and as low as 52-1/8. In each case there was a buyer and a seller.

The figure immediately to the right of the name indicates the company's estimated annual dividend rate of $1.45 per share. This estimate is based on the most recent quarterly payment and is an increase from the $1.35 per share the investor received from the company in 1975. Also, it is nearly three times greater than the dividend received when the stock was initially acquired about ten years earlier. Traditionally, the company has paid about half its earnings as dividends to stockholders and, fortunately, 3M's earnings have increased over the years.

The stock's "yield" of 2.6% can be calculated by dividing the $1.45 per share dividend by the current stock price. However, since the investor's shares were purchased at $27 back in 1965, the dividend yield is now better than 5% of the original capital invested ($1.45 per share divided by $27 per share).

The stock "closed" yesterday at 56-1/4 which means the last transaction of the day was at a price of $56.25. This was 1/2 of a point or 50 cents above the closing price of the day before. Throughout the entire trading session yesterday the stock was traded at prices ranging as low as 55-1/2 ($55.50) and as high as 56-3/8 ($56.375).

The stock of Minnesota Mining is listed not only on the New York Stock Exchange but also on the Boston and Cincinnati stock exchanges. Yesterday, 72,500 shares were traded (72,500 shares bought and 72,500 shares sold). Because the New York Stock Exchange is the largest exchange, most of the 72,500 shares traded were probably bought and sold on the trading floor in New York, but from these figures the reader cannot be sure.

The price/earnings ratio, also called the P/E ratio, measures the relationship between the current price of the stock and the company's earnings per share. It is calculated by dividing the current price of the stock by the earnings per share. Based on the closing price of Minnesota Mining yesterday (56-1/4) and the earnings per share reported by the company over the past twelve months (not shown), the P/E ratio is 23, as it appears in the middle column.

It should be noted that the P/E multiple is always in a state of flux. In this case, since this 1976 example, 3M's P/E ratio has declined because the company's earnings progress has been better than the stock performance.

Stock Market Activity At the top of the stock table is a special market activity section that shows total shares traded, called "volume," and highlights the ten or fifteen most active stocks of the day. Volume is important, but investors should not be concerned if a particular stock is on, or not on, the most active list. A stock can rise or fall on high or low volume.

The number of shares traded during the day is totaled by each exchange after it closes. However, the total volume of the New York Stock Exchange is the figure used most often by news commentators to describe the day's market activity.

In the early 1920's a very active day on the New York exchange was a total of 1,500,000 shares traded. By the late 1920's daily volume of 4,000,000 shares was not unusual. The panic in October, 1929 produced several days of high volume (the record 16,410,000 shares traded on October 29, 1929 was not surpassed for nearly forty years). Since the 1950's, volume has steadily increased due principally to a larger number of companies and shares, not to mention greater activity by institutions (mutual funds, pension funds, insurance companies and banks). On August 26, 1982, a record 137,330,000 shares changed hands. Today, a total daily volume of 45,000,000 shares is considered normal.

28 THE WALL STREET JOURNAL

Thursday's Volume
23,277,430 Shares; 38,200 Warrants

TRADING BY MARKETS

	Shares	Warrants
New York Exchange	19,850,000	37,500
Midwest Exchange	1,025,400	....
Pacific Exchange	737,600	....
Nat'l Assoc. of Securities Dealers	1,051,530	700
Philadelphia Exchange	322,200	....
Boston Exchange	227,000	....
Detroit Exchange	1,800	....
Cincinnati Exchange	56,600	....
Instinet System	5,300	....

New York Stock Exchange

Volume since Jan. 1:	1976	1975	1974
Total shares	2,849,135,941	2,599,034,070	1,668,436,835
Total warrants	14,727,400	61,325,300	13,784,400

MOST ACTIVE STOCKS

	Open	High	Low	Close	Chg.	Volume
Am Tel&Tel	56	56½	55⅝	56⅜	+ ⅝	344,700
Xerox Cp	60¼	61⅜	60	61¼	+1½	260,900
Tenneco	31⅜	32	31⅜	32	+ ¾	189,500
Phillips Pet	60	61⅛	59	60½	− ⅜	185,900
IntTelTel	27⅞	28¼	27¾	28⅛	+ ½	169,900
AmCred wi	12¾	13¼	12¾	13¼	+ ⅜	159,200
Am Cyan	24⅝	24¾	24⅛	24⅛	− ⅜	157,400
Tampa Elec	16½	16⅝	16½	16⅝	......	154,500
Singer Co	21⅞	23½	21¾	23⅜	+1⅞	152,700
Texaco Inc	27⅜	27⅝	27¼	27⅜	+ ⅛	140,500

MARKET DIARY

	Fri	Thur	Wed	Tues	Mon	(a)
Issues traded	1,906	1,901	1,866	1,910	1,879	2,094
Advances	919	1,165	963	900	808	1,431
Declines	543	353	469	543	579	443
Unchanged	444	383	434	467	492	220
New highs	86	76	49	42	23	158
New lows	15	8	21	21	37	75

(a) Summary for the week

Market Breadth In addition to using stock market averages, the general market trend can be seen by glancing at the "market breadth" figures usually found in the "Market Diary" column near the stock tables. These figures, available for the NYSE as well as the other markets, show the number of stocks that advanced or declined each day as well as the number of stocks that reached new high or low prices for the year. While these statistics have only limited value on a day-to-day basis, they become more significant as trends are established over a period of time.

Wall Street professionals often say "it is a market of stocks rather than a stock market" and, to some extent, this is true. It is not unusual to see a stock or a group of stocks contrarily hit new highs in a bear market or sink to new lows in a bull market. However, a broad stock market advance or decline can be a powerful influence on an individual stock. For this reason, it pays to keep abreast of the condition or trend of the overall market.

Earnings Reports Over the long term — a few years or longer — the price of a stock will most likely rise or fall in line with the company's earnings, dividends and financial condition. Consequently, there is a tendency for investors to anticipate future earnings reports which, in turn, places some importance on earnings announcements.

A company usually reports its sales and earnings results every three months. In most cases, the figures are available a few weeks after the quarter ends. A majority, but not all, of the companies end their business year on December 31, the end of the regular calendar year. If December 31 is used (rather than a "fiscal year" that ends on another month), the first quarter would close on March 31, the second quarter on June 30, and the third quarter on September 30. These quarterly statements are referred to as "interim reports." A company's year is comprised of three interim reports and one annual report.

A quarterly interim report is mailed to each shareholder almost immediately. However, a few of the pertinent figures will frequently appear over the news wires and in the newspaper two or three days before the report is actually received by the shareholder. Sometimes the earnings report is

Digest of Earnings Reports

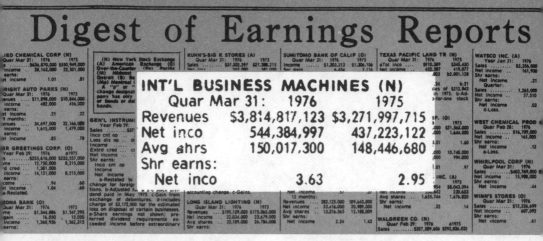

better or worse than Wall Street expects and this can produce an immediate positive or negative price change in the stock. Although most long term investors do not buy or sell stocks based solely on quarterly results, short term traders are sometimes influenced by these reports.

Most major newspapers publish company sales and earnings announcements. The *Wall Street Journal* devotes considerable space to these reports in a daily column entitled "Digest of Earnings Reports" which usually appears near the middle of the paper.

The 1976 first quarter announcement of International Business Machines Corporation is a good example. The company's report, published in the Earnings Digest column of the *Journal* in mid-April, is shown above.

This brief report tells the reader that, in the three month period ending March 31, 1976, IBM sold or rented more than $3.8 billion of computers and other business products compared with almost $3.3 billion in the same three month period a year earlier. The report also shows that IBM enjoyed earnings of about $544 million or $3.63 per share in the first quarter which compares favorably with the $437 million net profit or $2.95 earnings per share in the first quarter of 1975.

Of course, not all companies have the benefit of publicity with each quarterly report, but IBM is a widely-held stock. While this announcement appeared quite favorable, the story, as shown on the next page, explained the company's report in greater detail. It also described the immediate reaction of Wall Street.

Investors frequently interpret a company's interim report positively when the quarterly comparison is better than the preceding quarterly comparison and view it negatively when the reverse occurs. Stated differently, investors like to see earnings improve — especially at an increasing rate.

IBM's Net Rose 25% to a Record In First Quarter

Total Revenue Climbed 17% As Firm's Outright Sales Continued at High Level

By a WALL STREET JOURNAL Staff Reporter

ARMONK, N.Y.—International Business Machines Corp.'s net income in the first quarter jumped nearly 25% from a year before to a record $544.4 million, or $3.63 a share, as outright sales of its products continued at a high level.

Total revenue from sales and rentals rose nearly 17% to a record $3.81 billion.

However, Frank T. Cary, IBM's chairman and chief executive officer, again cautioned that the high proportion of outright sales isn't expected to continue. "Therefore," he said, "year-to-year comparisons in gross income (revenue) and net earnings throughout the remainder of 1976 are unlikely to be as favorable as those in the (first) quarter."

Sales of computers and other products bring IBM immediate profit and complete revenue, in contrast to rental, which spreads the return over several years. Most IBM data-processing products are rented to customers.

Outright Sales

In 1975, though, IBM's outright sales rose steadily from quarter to quarter from a relatively low level in the first period to a record $1.52 billion in the fourth.

In this year's first quarter, sales of all products declined from the fourth quarter to $1.29 billion, but that figure was nearly 44% higher than sales in the first quarter of 1975. As a result, sales accounted for nearly 34% of total revenue, compared with 27% a year before.

Revenue from rentals and services in the first quarter rose 6.4% from a year before to $2.53 billion and accounted for 66% of total revenue, compared with 73% a year before.

The growth rate of rental and service revenue in the first quarter was well under the 14% of the fourth quarter and the 18% achieved for all of 1975.

Besides the high proportion of outright sales, an IBM spokesman said, foreign-currency translation was a factor in the lower growth rate of rental and service revenue.

Year-Earlier Results

IBM earned $437.2 million, or $2.95 a share, on total revenue of $3.27 billion in the first quarter of 1975. Those figures set company records at the time, but were affected by the recession. Net rose only 1% on a 9% revenue increase.

This year's first quarter results were the second best for any quarter in IBM's history. The records came in the fourth quarter of 1975, when IBM earned $588.6 million, or $3.94 a share, on revenue of $4.07 billion. In reporting on that fourth quarter, Mr. Cary said the "accelerating trend" in outright sales wasn't expected to continue in 1976.

Yesterday, Mr. Cary said incoming orders for data-processing equipmnent "increased significantly" in the first quarter from a year earlier, "reflecting the general improvoment in the ocoonomio olimate." He said shipments of IBM equipment "also compared favorably" with the year-earlier period's.

IBM's "other income," principally interest, rose 16% to $107 million in the first quarter from $92.2 million a year before, after having fallen more than 8% from a year before in the fourth quarter to $109.5 million.

Analysts' Forecasts

In January, IBM's fourth quarter report was better than many securities analysts had expected, and the New York Stock Exchange halted trading for a while before the stock picked up a gain for the day of $2.375 a share.

Yesterday, the reverse was true. Good as it was, IBM's per-share earnings report of $3.63 was under many analysts' forecasts of $3.65 to $3.80.

In trading on the New York Stock Exchange, IBM sold as low as $261.50 a share after its earnings report was released and closed at $262, down $5.75 from Friday's close. Before the earnings statement, IBM had traded as high as $270.75 a share, up $3 from Friday's close.

74

Dividend news, good or bad, can
be important to stockholders.

Dividends and Stock Splits Each quarter a company's board of directors meets to decide how much, if any, earnings will be paid to stockholders as a cash dividend. If a dividend is "declared," the directors will also set a "date of record." This means stockholders on record on or before that date are entitled to this dividend. Anybody buying the stock after that date would have to wait for the next declaration to receive a dividend. As a result, the stock's market price is reduced by the amount of the dividend on the day after the date of record. To say it another way, the stock is "ex-dividend" after that date.

When a company's earnings improve, the directors might raise the regular dividend rate or, perhaps, declare an "extra dividend." This term is not to be confused with the term "ex-dividend." On the other hand, if the company's earnings trend is unfavorable, the dividend could be reduced or omitted entirely. Dividend announcements, good or bad, can be found in a special dividend section of the newspaper as shown on the next page.

Sometimes the directors of a corporation will want to conserve cash but still reward the stockholders. In this instance, the directors might declare a "stock dividend." As an example, a stockholder who owns 100 shares of a company declaring a 10% stock dividend would receive another 10 shares from the company — although the value of all 110 shares would be the same as the 100 shares held initially. The pie is simply being divided into eleven pieces rather than ten. If the company's per share cash dividend rate remains the same, the stockholder has, in effect, been given increased future dividend income. However, if the dividend rate is cut to adjust for the stock dividend or if the company does not pay a regular cash dividend and has no intention of doing so, then the stockholder has received absolutely nothing new. In this case, the directors of the company should explain their action to the stockholders.

Much the same can be said about a "stock split" regardless of how the stock is divided — 2 for 1, 3 for 1, 3 for 2 or whatever. For example, if XYZ Company has 2,000,000 shares outstanding and the directors declare a 2 for 1 stock split, there would be 4,000,000 shares or twice as many outstanding after the split. If the stock price happened to be $50 before, it would be $25 after. At the same time, the earnings per

Corporate Dividend News

AT&T's Quarterly Is Raised 10 Cents, To 95 Cents a Share

By a WALL STREET JOURNAL Staff Reporter

NEW YORK — American Telephone & Telegraph Co. raised its quarterly common stock dividend 10 cents, to 95 cents a share, payable April 1 to stock of record March 2.

The dividend increase, which will mean the annual payout on the most widely held corporate stock will rise to $3.80 a share from $3.40, had been expected by some analysts despite the per-share earnings drop AT&T posted in 1975. Chairman John D. deButts said the rise "reflects the directors' confidence in the economy's continuing recovery and in our own business's prospects."

AT&T net income fell to $3.15 billion, or $5.13 a share, in 1975, from $3.17 billion, or $5.85 a share, the year before, the company reported a few weeks ago. The drop resulted from poor earnings by AT&T's Western Electric Co. unit. Mr. deButts said yesterday that long-distance calling and new phone installations are growing at a faster pace.

The added payout on the 582,023,866 common shares AT&T had outstanding at year-end will cost the company $232.8 million a year.

* * *

Halliburton Directors Boost Quarterly Payout, Clear 3-for-1 Stock Split

By a WALL STREET JOURNAL Staff Reporter

DALLAS — Halliburton Co. said its directors approved a three-for-one split of its common stock and increased the quarterly cash dividend payment to 42 cents a share from 33 cents a share.

The company will distribute two additional shares April 29 for each share of record March 29. The cash dividend for the first quarter will be paid March 23 on stock of record March 5.

Halliburton said the new annual presplit dividend rate of $1.68 a share represents a 27% increase from the previous rate of $1.32 a share. After the split, the annual and quarterly dividend rates will be 56 cents a share and 14 cents a share, respectively.

The engineering and construction company has 19,484,694 shares of common stock issued.

Company	Period	Amt.	Payable date	Record date
Am Tel & Tel $4pf	Q	1.00	5– 1–76	3–31
Atlantic Steel Co		.17½	4– 1–76	3–13
Babson Income Trust		h.03	2–27–76	2–19
Calif Portland Cem	Q	.25	4–12–76	3–16
Chesebrough-Pond's Inc	Q	c.38	3–25–76	3– 4
Chesebrough-Pond's Inc		p		6– 4
p-Two-for-one stock split, subject to approval May 6, 1976.				
Clausing Corp		c.16	3–19–76	3– 5
Coastal St Gas $1.19pfA	Q	.29¾	3–15–76	2–25
Coastal St Gas $1.83pfB	Q	.45¾	3–15–76	2–25
Cont'l BAnk Norristown	Q	.42	3–15–76	3– 1
CPL Corp	Yr-end	.40	4– 1–76	3–10
Crown Zellrbh Canada		.30	3–12–76	2–27
El Paso Electric Co	Q	.23	3–15–76	2–27
Elizabethtown Water Co	Q	.55	3–31–76	3–15
Evans Inc		.15	3–15–76	2–27
1st Int'l Bancshares		.27½	3–31–76	3–17
Genstar Ltd	Q	.30	3–23–76	3– 2
Homasote Co	Q	.06	3–15–76	2–27
Intl Courier Corp	Q	.06	4–15–76	3–31
Kollmorgen Corp	Q	c.12½	3–11–76	3– 1
Merchants Nat'l Corp	Q	.20	3–19–76	3– 1
Morse Shoe Inc	Q	.07½	4– 1–76	3– 5
Nat'l Steel Corp	Q	.62½	3–15–76	3– 1
Niag Moh Pwr 10.60%pf	Q	2.65	3–31–76	2–25
Niag Moh Pwr 11¾%pf	Q	2.93¾	3–31–76	2–25
NLT Corp	Q	.16	3–19–76	3– 5
Noranda Mines Ltd	Q	d.30	3–15–76	2–23
Norcen Energy Res Ltd	Q	.17	3– 1–76	2–25
Northeast Investrs Tr		.31	2–20–76	2–20
Northrop Corp new	Q	.30	3–20–76	3– 1
Northrop Cp $1.45pf	Q	.36¼	4– 7–76	3–19
Noxell Corp	Q	c.12	4– 1–76	3–18
Opelika Mfg Co	Q	.25	4– 5–76	3–15
Pilgrim Group:				
Magma Income Trust		h.14	3–15–76	2–17
Pratt-Read Corp	Q	.07½	3–15–76	2–27
PS Co No Carolina	Q	c.26	4– 1–76	3–10
Public Serv E&G Co	Q	.43	3–31–76	3– 1
Public Serv E&G $1.40pf	Q	.35	3–31–76	3– 1
Public Serv E&G 4.08%pf	Q	1.02	3–31–76	3– 1
Realty Income Trust		.15	3–15–76	2–27
Reed Shaw Osler	Q	.07	3–15–76	3– 1
Reeves Bros Inc	Q	.45	3–15–76	3– 1
Revco DS Inc		.10	3–19–76	3– 5
St Paul Securities	M	.08	3–15–76	2–27
Servomation Corp	Q	.16½	6–10–76	5–10
Spang Indus Inc	S	.10	2–17–76	3– 2
Steelmet Inc	Q	.06	4–29–76	4–15
Union Special Corp	Q	.25	3–19–76	3– 3
Valspar Corp	Q	.06	4–15–76	4– 1
Wean Utd 5¼%pfA		n.31½	3–15–76	2–27
Wean Utd 5¼%pfA		n.31¼	3–15–76	2–27

* * *

Dividends Reported February 17

Company	Period	Amt.	Payable date	Record date
Aberdeen Mfg Corp	Q	.10	3–19–76	2–27
Aberdeen Mfg Corp	Stk	5%	3–19–76	2–27
Amer District Teleg Co	Q	c.16	3–19–76	2–27
Amer Utility Shares		h.19	3– 5–76	2–27
Banc Oklahoma Corp	Q	.25	3–18–76	3– 5
Barber Oil Corp	Q	.40	4– 1–76	3–12
Beneficial Std Corp	Q	.05	3–12–76	2–27
Broward Bancshares Inc	Q	.10	3–15–76	3– 1
Capitol Food Indus	Q	.04	4– 1–76	3–15
Carriers & Gen'l Corp	Q	.06⅛	3–15–76	3– 1
Century Tel Enter Inc	Q	c.08½	3–15–76	3– 1
Charter New York Corp	Q	.50	3–31–76	3– 1
Citizens & Sat'l Bk	Q	.13	3–15–76	2–27
Clow Corp	Q	.10	4–20–76	4– 2
Colt Indus $1.60pf A	Q	.40	3–31–76	3–15
Colt Indus $4.25pf D	Q	1.06¼	3–31–76	3–15
Con Nat Gas 10.96%pf	Q	2.74	4– 1–76	3–15
Cooper Industries Inc	Q	c.42	3–18–76	3– 4
Cooper Industries Inc		w	3–18–76	3– 4
w-Two-for-one stock split.				
Crocker Nat'l Corp	Q	.41½	4–15–76	3– 8
Crocker Nat'l $3pf	Q	.75	4–15–76	3–19
Daniel Int'l Corp	Q	.17½	3–29–76	3– 8
Donaldson Lufkin & Jenrt		.05	3–18–76	2–27
Egan Machinery Co	Q	.05	3–19–76	2–27
First City Bancorp Tex.	Q	c.25	3–15–76	3– 5
First Farwest Corp		p	3– 1–76	
pp-One-for-five reverse stock split subject to shareholders approval on June 1, 1976.				
First Hartford Cp srApf		.13	2–28–76	2–24
First Maryland Bancorp	Q	.34	4– 1–76	3– 5
First National Stores Inc	Q	.25	3–19–76	3– 1
Florida Gas Co	Q	.22½	3–15–76	3– 1
Foodways National Inc	In	.20	3–31–76	3–10
General Ohio S&L Corp	Q	.04	3–31–76	3– 8
Girard Co	Q	.81	4– 1–76	3– 1
Gulf Oil Canada	Q	h.25	4– 1–76	3–22

Company	Period	Amt.	Payab date
Havatampa Corp	Q	c.11	3–15–
Honeywell Inc	Q	.35	3–15–
Imperial Grp Ltd ADR	F	y	4–15–
y-Approx $.047 per depositary share.			
Joslyn Mfg & Supply Co	Q	.28	3–16–
Joslyn Mfg & Supply Co	E	.05	3–16–
Kelly Services Inc	Q	c.20	3–12–
Kelly Services Inc	Q	c.20	3–12–
Keystone Custodian Fds:			
Cust B-1		.12	3–15–
Cust B-4		h.18	3–15–
Cust S-1		.11	3–15–
Laneco Inc		.04	3–15–
Life Ins Co of Georgia	Q	c.20	3–10–
Lincoln Inco Life Insur	Q	.15	3–16–
Lincoln Inco Life Insur	E	.15	3– 1–
MacDermid Inc	Q	.12	4– 1–
Manhattan Life Corp	Q	c.06	3–15–
ManhattanLife Ins Co		.34	3–12–
Marshall & Ilsley Corp	Q	.50	3–12–
Maryland Nat Corp	Q	.18	3–31–
Modern Merchandising Inc Stk		25%	4–30–
Modern Merchandising Inc	In	.04	4–30–
Munsingwear Inc	Q	.27	3–15–
Nat'l Aviation Under	Q	.13	3–13–
Nat'l Presto Indus Inc	Q	.30	3–31–
Niagara Mohawk Pwr Corp	Q	.31	3–31
Niagara Mo Pwr 3.40%pf	Q	.85	3–31–
Niagara Mo Pwr 3.60%pf	Q	.90	3–31–
Niagara Mo Pwr 3.90%pf	Q	.97½	3–31–
Niagara Mo Pwr 4.10%pf	Q	1.02½	3–31–
Niagara Mo Pwr 4.85%pf	Q	1.12¼	3–31–
Niagara Mo Pwr 5.25%pf	Q	1.31¼	3–31–
Niagara Mo Pwr 6.10%pf	Q	1.52½	3–31–
Niagara Mo Pwr 7.72%pf	Q	1.93	3–31–
Niagara Mo Pwr 10.60%pf	Q	2.65	3–31–
Niagara Mo Pwr 11¾%pf	Q	2.93¾	3–31–
Noranda Mines Ltd	Q	d.30	3–15–
Ohio Edison Co	Q	.41½	3–31–
Ohio Edison 3.90%pf	Q	.97½	4– 1–
Ohio Edison 4.40%pf	Q	1.10	4– 1–
Ohio Edison 4.44%pf	Q	1.11	4– 1–
Ohio Edison 7.24%pf	Q	1.81	3–29–
Ohio Edison 7.36%pf	Q	1.84	3–15–
Ohio Edison 10.48%pf	Q	2.62	3–18
Overmyer Corp		.07	4– 1–
Owens-Illinois $4.75pf	Q	1.18¾	4– 1–
Phila National Corp	Q	.52½	4– 1–
Property Trust of Amer		(Omitted common)	
Public Serv E&G Co	Q	.43	3–31–
Pub Serv E&G $1.40pf	Q	.35	3–31–
Pub Serv E&G 4.08%pf	Q	1.02	3–31–
Pub Serv E&G 4.18%pf	Q	1.04½	3–31–
Pub Serv E&G 4.30%pf	Q	1.07½	3–31–
Pub Serv E&G 5.05%pf	Q	1.26¼	3–31–
Pub Serv E&G 5.28%pf	Q	1.32	3–31–
Pub Serv E&G 6.80%pf	Q	1.70	3–31–
Pub Serv E&G 7.40%pf	Q	1.85	3–31–
Pub Serv E&G 7.52%pf	Q	1.88	3–31–
Pub Serv E&G 7.70%pf	Q	1.92½	3–31–
Pub Serv E&G 7.80%pf	Q	1.95	3–31–
Pub Serv E&G 8.08%pf	Q	2.02	3–31–
Pub Serv E&G 9.62%pf	Q	2.40½	3–31–
Pub Serv E&G 9.75%pf	v	.6635	3–31–
v-Covers period from December 23, 1975 to			
1976.			
Pub Serv E&G 12.25%pf	Q	3.06¼	3–31–
Reynolds & Reynolds Co	Q	.10	4–12–
Royster Co	Q	.15	4– 1–
Salem Corp	Stk	4%	5– 3–
Salem Corp	Stk	4%	5– 3–
Secur Life & Accld Denver	Q	.11	3–12–
Simkins Indus Inc	Q	.15	4– 1–
Solon Auto Svcs Inc	Q	.02	3–19–
Stauffer Chemical Co		†	5– 27–
Stauffer Chem Co new	nn	c.33½	6– 2
t-Two-for-one stock split subject to shareholder approval on April 21, 1976. nn-The new payment will be 32½ cents.			
US Financial Corp	Q	.14	4–20
Victory Markets Inc	Q	.05	3–15–
Wash Real Est Inv Tr	Q	.32½	3–31–
Wells Fargo & Co	Q	.24	4–20

c-Increased dividend. d-Reduced dividend. e-Declared or paid so far this year. f-Paid in Canadian funds. k-From capital gains. b-Payable in installments. a, annual; Ac, accumulation; E, extra; G, interim; In, initial; Liq, liquidation; M, monthly; Q, quarterly; R, resumed; S, semi-annual; Sp, special.

* * *

Stocks Ex-Dividend Februar

Company	Amount	Company
AmStd $4.75pf	1.18	Nat'l Medical Enter
Castle & Cooke	.20	Norton Co
Deseret Pharmaceutl	.06¼	Potomac El Pwr
MBPXL Corp	k	Tex Pac LdTrSubS
k-10% stock.		

— H—H—H —

36	27⅛	Hack W	2.48	7	1	32⅝	32⅝	32⅝—	⅛
18⅝	14¾	HallFB	.60	13	74	17⅝	17⅜	17½+	⅛
17¼	13¾	HallPrt	.80a	7	5	15¼	15⅛	15¼--	⅛
166	133½	Hallibtn	1.68	13	373	155½	153	153⅜+	¾

Before the "when issued" period 3/24/76

— H—H—H —

36	27⅛	Hack W	2.48	7	3	32⅞	32½	32½—	⅛
18⅝	14¾	HallFB	.60	13	40	17½	17¼	17½......	
17¼	13¾	HallPrt	.80a	7	18	15½	15⅛	15¼......	
166	133½	Hallibtn	1.68	13	230	152½	150¾	151½—	1⅞
....		Hallibrtn	wi	...	1	51⅛	51⅛	51⅛......	

The new stock's first day of trading 3/25/76

share figure is also halved. A stockholder owning 100 shares before the split would, of course, own 200 shares after, but the total value would be the same (similar to holding two nickels instead of one dime). In other words, unless the dividend is increased, the stockholder receives nothing new when a company's stock is split.

There is, however, a school of thought that a lower priced stock becomes more "marketable" or more attractive to the investing public. To a certain degree, there is some truth to this. For psychological reasons primarily, some investors prefer owning stock in denominations of 100 shares, called "round lots," rather than any amount less than 100 shares, called "odd lots." It is a common belief by many investors that 3,000 shares of a $5 stock will appreciate in value more rapidly than 1000 shares of a $15 stock or 50 shares of a $300 stock. While it is true that a lower priced stock is often more volatile, the company's earnings progress is, by far, a more important influence on the future value of the stock.

Inexperienced investors can be misled by stock splits or, for that matter, by low priced stocks in general. A $20 stock is not necessarily a better buy than a $30 stock. In fact, the higher priced stock is frequently the leading company in its industry.

For example, there is IBM in the office equipment field, GM among the auto companies, Delta among the airlines, Eastman Kodak in photography, Alcoa Aluminum, Johnson & Johnson and so on. While all of these stocks have split at one time or another, the managements of these and other leading companies are probably fully aware of the informal status accorded the highest priced stock in the industry.

Ordinarily when a company—especially an important company—announces a stock split, the newspapers provide all the necessary details. Rarely does a split go unnoticed since there is a transitional period of a few weeks or so between the time the old stock is traded and the new, split shares are traded. During this period, the split stock is traded on a "when issued" basis which means the shares have been authorized by the corporation but not yet issued or delivered.

The illustrations above show how a split appears in the newspaper using the sequence of Halliburton Company's April, 1976, 3 for 1 stock split as an example. The company's split announcement appears on page 75.

– H–H–H –

36	27⅛	Hack W	2.48	7	5	32¾	32¼	32¾	......
18⅝	14¾	HallFB	.60	12	10	17⅝	17	17	− ⅝
17¼	13¾	HallPrt	.80a	6	2	14⅝	14⅝	14⅝	− ⅛
166	133½	Hallibtn	1.68	13	155	152¼	150⅜	150¾	− ¾
52⅛	48¼	Hallibrtn	wi	...	60	50⅞	50½	50¾	+ ⅛

The last day of the "when issued" period 4/29/76

– H–H–H –

36	27⅛	Hack W	2.48	7	4	33	32½	33	+ ¼
18⅝	14¾	HallFB	.60	12	35	17⅛	16½	16¾	− ¼
17¼	13¾	HaliPrt	.80a	7	11	15⅜	14¾	15⅜	+ ¾
52⅛	48¼	Hallibrt	n.56	13	562	50¼	49¾	50¼	− ½

The "new" stock is trading alone 4/30/76

Short Interest One popular Wall Street trading technique is "short selling" or "selling a stock short." When an investor expects a stock to *rise,* it is purchased with an intention of selling it later at a higher price. On the other hand, if the price is expected to *decline,* the shares can legally be "sold short" by borrowing them from a broker and then immediately selling them on the open market. The short seller must buy an equivalent number of shares back later, hopefully at a lower price. Once repurchased, the same number of shares are repaid to the broker. The profit, or the difference between the price at which the stock was sold and the price at which it was later purchased, belongs to the short seller (less commissions and taxes, of course).

At mid-month, each exchange announces its short interest figures. This is a list of companies showing, individually, the number of shares that had been sold short and were still short as of the indicated date, usually the 14th or 15th. For the most part, these are shares that must be repurchased in the future. It can be said that a high short interest is both bearish (because many believe stock prices will be declining) and bullish (because these shares represent potential buying power).

The Interpretation of Business News The social, economic and political circumstances of each market are never exactly the same, although "old timers" occasionally cite similarities. Nevertheless, an investor can be well informed on the financial events of the day by focusing on two principal news subjects: *the business cycle* and *inflation.*

The business cycle, which describes the expansion or contraction of the economy as a whole, has an important influence on the earnings trends of most companies. To keep abreast, there are eight key items the investor should watch:

- Trends in consumer confidence and spending.
- Actions by the Federal Reserve Board to tighten or ease the supply of money.
- The trend of interest rates (the "prime lending rate" is a good benchmark).
- The Government's Index of Leading Indicators.
- Tax increases or tax cuts.
- The accumulation or liquidation of business inventories.
- Capital expenditure plans of businesses for new plant and equipment.
- Government spending for defense and social needs.

LINDBERGH IS IN PARIS
PROHIBITION ENDED
THE WAR IS OVER
Astronauts Walk On The Moon

Inflation, the declining value of money due to rising prices, is caused, many economists believe, by excessive government spending. This subject should also be closely monitored because it influences, and is influenced by, the business cycle. Moreover, inflation has a direct impact on the investment environment. A rising or declining inflation rate can shift the balance of investment returns between stocks, bonds and other alternatives.

Finally, the investor should be alert for unusual opportunities. History contains many examples of how unexpected events can affect stock prices. By definition, unexpected events cannot be predicted, but they sometimes present an opportunity to profitably buy or sell against the emotions of the crowd.

Investing
and
trading

Introduction Noted financier Bernard M. Baruch once said "there is no investment which does not involve some risk and is not something of a gamble." Indeed, most experienced investors can immediately recognize the relationship between the risk level of a security and the reward it promises.

Because individuals' investment needs and objectives are different, their risk and reward expectations are different and their approaches to the stock market are different.

This chapter will help the new investor enter the Wall Street arena. It will aid in the selection of a stockbroker and provide guidelines to help the investor establish a realistic investment objective. In addition, it examines many stock market details serious investors should know. Explanations of the margin account, bear market strategies, arbitraging, a preliminary look at taxes, investment clubs and mutual funds are among the topics discussed.

Family Financial Planning Financial advisors unanimously recommend against buying common stocks, preferred stocks or long term bonds at least until:

(1) Some money has been set aside to meet emergency family needs for a few months or longer.

(2) An adequate property, health and life insurance plan has been established.

(3) Provisions have been made for other obvious needs such as a home, education and retirement.

The money earmarked for investing is frequently referred to as "risk capital" — no matter how conservative the intended investment program might be. Although the degree of risk can be controlled to some extent, an investor should use only that capital which can be called "discretionary." Also, advisors often recommend against committing the entire amount at any one time. A flexible investment program provides considerable peace of mind.

Besides money, time is also a factor. Managing a portfolio properly requires a certain amount of time and effort. A stockholder survey conducted a few years ago indicated that many investors spend six to twelve hours monthly on investment work.

For specific, personal advice on family financial planning, it would be best to consult either an attorney, an accountant or a banker, all being somewhat impartial observers. But, at this point, it should be remembered that nearly everyone is trying to sell something.

A well-organized financial plan will reveal exactly how much risk capital can or should be made available. With this family program complete, a personalized "investment objective" can then be established to determine the types of investments most suitable under the circumstances. Here, a good stockbroker can be worth his or her weight in gold.

The Stockbroker Searching for a stock-broker is much like looking for a family doctor. Expertise, personality and reputation are all important qualifications.

Ordinarily a stockbroker is referred by family, friends or business associates. It is best to begin the search with a candidate list of two or three people. The choice would be made following individual "interviews" (really nothing more than friendly conversations).

The person selected should be employed by a reputable brokerage firm, preferably a New York Stock Exchange member firm, and have experience or access to it. As a stockbroker for a member firm, the individual is most likely a graduate of an extensive training course and has passed a comprehensive test prepared by the New York Stock Exchange and the National Association of Securities Dealers before being approved by the Securities and Exchange Commission.

The rules and code of ethics are strict. Among the many regulations, a stockbroker is *forbidden* to guarantee any customer against a loss and cannot share in the profits or losses of any customer's account or rebate compensation to secure business.

Every broker interviewed will most likely appear as a friendly person in a busy, almost-hectic environment. The choice might be difficult. It is not unusual for a stockbroker to have two hundred or more customers, although probably no more than ten or fifteen might be considered extremely active. A broker is obviously on the phone much of the day and cannot devote too much time to only one client, so the interview should be brief — perhaps in the evening.

Other items to consider during the interviews are personality, investment philosophy, quality of the firm's research, other services and, of course, the level of commission rates. Sometimes, but not often, paperwork in the "back office" of a well-managed brokerage firm can result in clerical errors. Discussions with other people who use the brokerage firms being considered is one way to check the frequency of this possible inconvenience.

Once all interviews have been completed and the selection has been made, a conference should be held between the customer and the broker to review the client's investment objective. If personal finances are discussed, the topics might include age and family circumstances, income, personal debt, interest payments, insurance coverage and inheritance, if any. As suggested earlier, it is advisable to have all family financial planning completed beforehand.

The brokerage firm charges a modest commission each time stock is bought and sold. The stockbroker, an employee of the firm, will receive a portion of that fee. For example, the commission on the purchase or sale of 100 shares of a $30 stock, a $3,000 investment, is typically about $58 (about 1.9%) and, depending on the firm's policy, the stockbroker's share would be roughly $15-20. A stockbroker's income obviously increases if stock is bought and sold more frequently which, from a customer's standpoint, is sometimes counterproductive. This practice, taken to an extreme, is called "churning" and can result in severe penalties to the broker and the firm if they encourage it. This is not usually a problem. Stockbrokers know it is to their own advantage in the long run to help each customer become a successful investor.

Stockbrokers should not be judged by the short term price action of stocks recommended or not recommended (they can neither control stock prices nor consistently predict them). They should be judged primarily by the quality of service they provide for the commission dollars they are being paid.

To use a stockbroker most effectively, the investor should:

- Be considerate and call only when necessary rather than just to "chat." As a result, the stockbroker will return a call more promptly thinking it must be important. To be fair, a small-commission customer should not demand a large slice of the broker's time.

- Listen to the stockbroker's advice. The ultimate decision to buy or sell, however, should rest entirely with the customer — the same person assuming the credit or the blame for each decision.

- Be explicit when placing an order or giving instructions to keep "misunderstandings" to a minimum. This is important because most business is conducted over the telephone.

- Look to the stockbroker as a valuable information source. The customer should feel free to ask for research reports and other investment data.

- Build a research library at home. Old stock guides, investment handbooks, annual reports and other research material kept in home files will make the job of searching for background information much easier later.

Drawing by Whitney Darrow, Jr.; ©1956
The New Yorker Magazine, Inc.

"Let me put it this way. It's five years from now. What am I kicking myself for not having bought?"

86

An artist's rendering of trading on the New York Stock Exchange in 1850.

Discount Brokers Most investors want or need the extra assistance and stockbroker relationships the so-called "full-service" brokerage firms provide. However, firms offering cut-rate commissions, referred to as "discount brokers," are worth considering if the investor expects to be independent and anticipates high commission costs.

An individual who trades no more than five or six times each year might find the 30% to 50% average saving insignificant in dollar terms. In some cases, discount brokers require a modest minimum annual amount or a deposit and, in most cases, there is a minimum transaction charge of $20-$30. But for an active investor trading fifteen or twenty times or more each year, the saving could be sizable.

Since May, 1975, when all fixed commission rates were abolished, the number of discount brokers has increased dramatically. Today, discount brokers can be found in many major cities. As with other aspects of investing, if a discount broker is being considered, it would be wise to investigate the firm and its background.

Opening an Account Opening a brokerage account is no more difficult than initiating a charge account at a local store or a checking account with a bank. In fact, they are similar in many ways. The individual must demonstrate a satisfactory credit rating, certain financial responsibilities must be met, the account can be personal or joint, and a monthly statement is mailed to the customer.

The typical stock brokerage office is a large room with ten to twenty desks for the brokers and a designated "gallery" area where customers can stand or sit to watch the ticker tape(s) on the wall that display stock prices. In addition, there is often a small library containing reference books, research reports and other investment material, plus a "Quotron" machine available for customers who want the latest stock quotes and a "broad tape" for up-to-the-minute news items.

Depending upon the policies of the firm or office manager, it is usually not necessary to have an account with the brokerage firm to visit the office. However, it is considered discourteous to be in the way of the firm's customers.

The day on which a share of stock is bought or sold is called the "trade date." The customer (and the broker) must deposit the required cash and/or securities into the

account on or before the fifth business day after the transaction takes place. This deadline is known as the "settlement date." Saturdays, Sundays and holidays are not included.

Once the brokerage firm has been paid in full for stock purchased, the new stockholder can request any one of three procedures:

(1) The stock can be "transferred and shipped." This means the name of the owner is transferred onto the stock certificate which is mailed to the designated address. This process, usually involving a transfer agent (e.g., a bank), normally takes about two weeks. The stockholder must then find a safe place to keep the certificate. If it is lost or destroyed it can, with some effort, be replaced.

(2) The stock can be "transferred and held." This means the certificate is prepared, as in the first case, but is kept for the owner in the brokerage firm's vault. If the stock is sold later, the owner must sign a "stock power" permitting transferral to the new owner.

(3) The stock can be held in "street name." In this instance, the stock is safely held by the broker in the broker's name for the customer's convenience. All divi-

dends, otherwise mailed directly from the company to the stockholder, are credited to the account or forwarded as the customer directs. Corporate reports and proxy statements (used for voting) are forwarded to the customer.

The monthly statement mailed to the customer is similar to a bank statement in appearance. It shows, in addition to other data, a beginning balance, all transactions made during the period, a final cash balance and stock positions at the end of the period. Stock held in the account at the date of the statement is said to be "long;" stock owed to the account by the customer is said to be "short."

There are two basic types of accounts — a cash account and a margin account. Many brokerage customers have both.

The cash account, by far the most popular, is used when securities are bought or sold in a direct cash transaction. In a cash account, every transaction is concluded on or before the settlement date. If stock has been purchased, the customer has paid for it in full, the customer's broker has paid the seller's broker and the shares have been credited to the buyer's account . . . all within five business days.

A margin account, which will be explained in greater detail later, allows the customer to borrow from the broker part of the amount needed to purchase or sell securities. The minimum New York Stock Exchange requirement is $2,000 to open a margin account in which most types of securities can be bought and sold. The margin account, like the cash account, demands that all transactions be concluded by a settlement date, but a customer buying or selling "on margin" need not deposit more than the required amount by that time. The broker will extend some credit to the customer based on the amount of cash and/or securities in the account. For this service, the customer pays an interest charge to the broker.

Because a minor does not have the legal power to contract in his or her own name, opening a brokerage account is limited to adults. Until the mid-1950's, giving securities to minors and having shares registered in a minor's name presented complications. Since then, to deal with this problem, all states have adopted laws similar in most cases to the 1956 Uniform Gifts to Minors Act sponsored by the brokerage industry. Under these laws, minors can own securities in special "custodial accounts" if the minor also has an adult custodian (most likely an adult family member). The laws are different in many states. It is, therefore, advisable to know the law and its possible disadvantages before a custodial account is opened.

Professional Counsel A professional investment advisor is worth considering if the individual has a large sum of money to invest, say $50,000-$70,000 or more, and has neither an interest in mutual funds (explained later) nor the time to devote to personal portfolio management. Advisory fees, which are usually tax-deductible, vary. The fee is typically 1-1½% annually on portfolios up to about $200,000. Thereafter, the cost declines proportionately. The investor must still pay brokerage commissions but may designate a stockbroker, give the counselor freedom to select the broker or instruct that orders be executed at the lowest possible commission rate. Most investment counselors work closely with several stockbrokers and a few banks.

In addition to investment counselors, trust departments of many banks also offer professional services. These services typically include both portfolio management and custodial functions, for essentially the same 1-1½% fee structure. Most investment counselors and banks either have in-house investment research or the ability to obtain it elsewhere. Custodial functions, such as safekeeping of securities, dividend or interest collection and disbursements, and other accounting tasks, are handled primarily by banks.

The recommended approach, at least initially, for persons employing professional money management services is a "non-discretionary" account with an understanding that the advisor has some freedom in managing the portfolio. In this way, the investor will be involved, can learn more about the investment process, and be in a better position to evaluate the style and talents of the portfolio manager.

Investment Objectives Selecting an objective that best meets an individual's personal financial needs is difficult. There are often many confusing alternatives.

Generally speaking, portfolios are managed for *income, capital appreciation,* or *safety,* or some combination thereof.

Risk and Reward

Perhaps the most basic of all Wall Street concepts is: "The greater the expected return, the greater the investment risk." In effect, the "risk/reward ratio," as it is often called, places a desire to preserve capital at one end of the spectrum and a desire to maximize return at the other end. Evidence of this principle has been documented in several thorough studies of historic rates of investment return. The table presented on the next page is based on these findings. It shows, in very general terms, the approximate risk/reward choices investors have had over the past several decades. Throughout this period, the rate of inflation averaged 2-4% annually.

It is important to note that this risk/reward table can change dramatically from one month to the next as investors respond to changes in interest rates or inflation. For example, given an inflation rate of 5.5%, U. S. Treasury Bills 4.5%, Savings Accounts 5.0% and Corporate Bonds 7.5%, one might conclude that a share of stock should provide a return of at least 10% to be competitive for the investor's dollar.

With the high interest and inflation rates experienced in recent years, it is easy to see why investors have become more sensitive to these relationships.

In addition, each category on the table obviously has its own risk/reward scale — and all opportunities relate to one another. There are, for example, many low-quality bonds that provide a better return (also with greater risk) than the typical high-quality stock.

Investment	Degree of Risk	Annual Return (Reward)
Treasury Bill	*Smallest degree of risk. Only the government has the power to print money. The return is usually just enough to offset inflation.*	2.5-3.5%
Government Bond	*High degree of safety. Adjusted for inflation, the return is modest.*	3.0-4.0%
Savings Account	*Greater risk than government bonds, although funds are insured by the government. Little protection against higher rates of inflation.*	3.5-4.5%
Corporate Bond	*More risk than a savings account. Priority over common stock if there is a business failure. Adjusted for inflation, the return is modest.*	4.0-5.0%
Share of Stock	*The highest degree of risk due to possible business failure. The return includes about 4% from dividends. Some protection from inflation.*	7.0-9.0%

Selection and Timing

To be successful on Wall Street, every investor must find a satisfactory combination of two key variables — *investment selection* and *investment timing.* While it may sound elementary and trite, an investor must make the proper selection at the proper time to obtain the best possible results. A wrong selection at the wrong time can be costly and mixed results can be obtained with any other combination.

As a general rule, investment selection and investment timing are inversely important. When the investment horizon is longer, selection becomes more important than timing. But timing becomes more important than selection when the investment horizon is shorter. For example, the common stock of Deere & Company, the leading manufacturer of farm equipment, is currently selling for about $30 per share. An investor who bought the stock at the equivalent price of $4 in May, 1957 is probably not overly concerned today that the stock could have been purchased at a much lower price in October, 1957. A short term trader, however, is *always* concerned with timing.

Total Return

Securities analysts often compare investment opportunities by estimating the total capital appreciation and dividend (or interest) return each investment can provide annually. This calculation, expressed as a total annual percentage figure, is referred to as "total return."

Done properly, total return takes into account possible tax consequences — especially when tax-free investments are under consideration. Because taxes are personal and unique to each investor, they are excluded in the examples to follow, however.

Future capital appreciation of a stock is difficult to estimate. To make the calculation easier, analysts assume in their total return assumptions that today's price/ earnings ratios will not be changing in the future. This means the estimated growth rate of earnings per share can be used in place of the capital appreciation estimate. Thus, a stock having a projected earnings per share growth rate of 8% and a current dividend yield of 3% has an expected total return of 11% before taxes.

Using the total return approach, an investor can immediately see what each in-

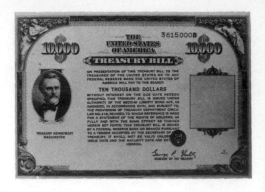

vestment offers. As an example, here is a hypothetical comparison:

	Possible Capital Appreciation	Dividend or Interest Yield	Total Return
"X" Growth Stock (Earnings Per Share Growth + Div. Yield)	10%	2%	12%
"Y" Income Stock (Earnings Per Share Growth + Div. Yield)	7%	5%	12%
"Z" Corporate Bond (Bond Discount to Maturity + Int. Yield)	2%	7%	9%*
Savings Account	0%	5%	5%
Treasury Bill	4%	0%	4%

*Also called "yield to maturity."

In this case, an investor comparing total return opportunities must make a value judgment between the highly assured 4% return of the treasury bill, a reasonably safe 5% return of the savings account, a less certain 9% return of the bond and a much less certain 12% return from either stock. To repeat, taxes must also be taken into consideration.

Finally, when comparing individual stocks of similar quality that offer the same total return, investors should realize that a growth stock probably represents higher initial market risk and greater reward over time than a slower-growing, higher-yielding stock. In the preceding example, both stocks promise the same total return of 12% but, based on the "bird-in-the-hand" argument, there might be greater assurance obtaining 12% from the income stock initially than from the growth stock. However, patient investors will find that future earnings increases of the growth stock will, within a few years, produce superior investment results overall.

The Margin Account In a land of credit
cards and financial conveniences and more
than 130 million adults, it is surprising there
are fewer than 1 million margin accounts
in use. While it is true the margin account is
sometimes complex and definitely not for
everybody, its application extends well
beyond the simple function of buying securities on credit. The margin account is a tool
that provides flexibility for the serious
investor.

Upon opening a margin account and sub-
mitting the normal credit information, the
investor will be asked to sign a margin
agreement and loan consent which will permit the brokerage firm to pledge or lend
securities carried for the account. In addition, the margin account will be subject
to various rules including, as mentioned
earlier, an *initial minimum requirement* of
the New York Stock Exchange, an *initial
margin requirement* established by Regu-
lation T of the Federal Reserve Board
(FRB), and *maintenance requirements*
enforced by the brokerage firm.

The initial margin requirement is the minimum percent of total value investors must
deposit to purchase or sell securities in a
margin account. The initial margin requirement for stocks (not all stocks qualify) has
been raised twelve times and lowered ten
times since the FRB was given power to

regulate security credit under the Securities Exchange Act in 1934. The margin requirement since 1934 has been as low as
40% (1937) and as high as 100% (1946). The
most recent Board action was in January,
1974 when the initial margin requirement
was lowered from 65% to 50%. In other
words, to make a $10,000 stock purchase in
a margin account today, an investor must
put up, within five days, at least $5,000 col-
lateral rather than $6,500 as it was before.

There is an easy way to calculate the
amount that can be bought with a specific amount of cash available:

*Add two zeros and divide
by the margin number.*

By applying this simple formula, an investor can quickly see that $6,000 cash will
buy $8,571 worth of marginable securities
when the margin requirement is 70%
($6,000 + 00 divided by 70); or $10,000 when
the margin is 60% ($6,000 + 00 divided by
60); or $12,000 when the margin is 50%
($6,000 + 00 divided by 50).

Using the figures in the last case as an example, if the margin requirement is 50% and the investor deposits $6,000 cash collateral, a decision to purchase, say, $9,000 of marginable stock would be recorded in the margin account in this manner:

$9,000 *Current Market Value*
 3,000 *Debit Balance*

$6,000 *Current Equity*
 4,500 *Required Margin* (50% X $9,000)

$1,500 *Excess Margin* (can be withdrawn or invested)

The $1,500 excess margin, if invested, has a "buying power" of $3,000 (i.e., $1,500 + 00 divided by 50) which, with the $9,000 already invested, would take the account up to its marginable limit of $12,000.

"Debit balance" is money the investor owes to the brokerage firm. For this service, the investor is charged an interest rate somewhat above the prime rate charged by banks. This cost should not be disregarded. Normally based on a daily average of the debit balance, the interest cost can fluctuate from month-to-month as interest rates swing. For example, in 1974, when the prime rate rose to about 12%, an investor's annual cost of carrying a debit balance could have been 14% or more. This is a high price to pay for stock market capital.

A margin account provides *leverage* which can expand or contract an investor's equity position quickly as the figures below demonstrate.

Continuing the earlier example, if the market value of the portfolio climbed 22% from $9,000 to $11,000, the investor's equity would increase 33% and buying power would be 67% greater.

$11,000 *Current Market Value*
 3,000 *Debit Balance*

$ 8,000 *Current Equity*
 5,500 *Required Margin* (50% X $11,000)

$ 2,500 *Excess Margin* ($5,000 buying power)

If, instead of rising, the value of the portfolio declined 22% to $7,000, the results would be quite different. In this case, equity declines 33% and buying power drops 67%.

$7,000 *Current Market Value*
 3,000 *Debit Balance*

$4,000 *Current Equity*
 3,500 *Required Margin* (50% X $7,000)

$ 500 *Excess Margin* ($1,000 buying power)

At most brokerage firms, the margin account is the responsibility of a centralized back office department, called the margin department. With the help of computers,

The curbstone brokers filling orders during a blizzard in the early 1900's.

these people review every account daily to keep the firm's stockbrokers and customers informed regarding certain guidelines. The first is a check to see whether a margin customer's equity is above or below the current Federal initial margin requirement, as explained earlier. If it has fallen below, the account is considered "restricted." In a restricted account, the investor has no additional buying power and cannot withdraw more than 30% of any sale proceeds. The remaining 70% would be retained to reduce the debit balance.

Another guideline closely watched is the maintenance requirement set by the New York Stock Exchange (NYSE) or by the brokerage firm itself which sometimes has a requirement more strict than that of the exchange. The NYSE maintenance requirement states that a customer's equity may at no time be less than 25% of the market value of securities carried (brokerage firms often set a 30% or 35% limit). If equity does drop below this level, the account is said to be "undermargined" and the customer will be asked to put up more margin. This is known as a "margin call." If more collateral is not deposited, the securities are sold by the broker.

The margin department will establish more than one type of margin account for a customer who uses margin for other specific

reasons such as selling stock short, buying or selling convertible bonds, buying or selling non-convertible bonds, etc. Moreover, margin requirements often vary for different types of securities. There are, in other words, many details investors should learn before using a margin account extensively. This information can be obtained from most brokerage firms or by writing to:

The New York Stock Exchange
11 Wall Street
New York, New York 10005

"Playing" the Market There are several tools and strategies that can lend versatility to an investment program and, in some cases, make stock market investing more profitable. While many of these techniques are not appropriate for conservative long term portfolios, all serious investors should at least be aware of the alternatives available.

Types of Orders

The *market order* to buy or sell is the most widely used type. It is simply an instruction to the stockbroker and others involved to buy or sell stock at the best possible price once the order reaches the trading post or trading desk. Normally, a market order is executed at a price reasonably close to the quote obtained before the order was entered. If the stock is volatile, however, the final price could be better or worse than expected. It normally takes only a few minutes to complete a market order transaction and report back to the stockbroker. In most cases, a confirmation slip is mailed to the investor within 24 hours.

The *limit order* is an instruction to buy or sell a stated amount of stock at a specific price (or better). When the target price is not within the current market quote, it is said to be "away from the market" and will be entered on the specialist's book beneath any similar orders received earlier. Therefore, if there are, as they say, "shares ahead of you," the limit order may not be executed immediately or maybe not at all at that price.

The *stop order,* called the *stop-loss order* many years ago, is a trading tool designed to protect a profit or prevent further loss if the stock begins to move in the wrong direction. This idea is based on the ageless Wall Street advice: "Let your profits run; cut your losses short." The stop order becomes a market order once the stock trades at or through a certain price, known as the "stop price." If the stop price is reached, there is no guarantee the executed price will be as favorable. It is possible, for example, to place an order to sell 100 shares of XYZ at

54 "stop" and later receive notice that your stock was sold at 53½. Except in technical analysis situations, the stop price should not be placed too close to the current market price since many stocks can randomly fluctuate 15% or more in a brief period of time. Long term investors will probably not need the stop order in the normal course of investing.

The *stop limit order* is a stop order and limit order combination. Like the stop order, it is a trading tool that requires extreme care. A stop limit order to <u>buy</u> means as soon as a trade occurs at the stop price or higher, the order becomes a limit order to buy. A stop limit order to <u>sell</u> works the same way. As soon as a trade occurs at the stop price or lower, the order becomes a limit order to sell.

Each order to buy or sell may be entered for a single trading day, week, month or it may be an *open order* — also called a *good 'til canceled (GTC) order.* An open order will remain in force until it is canceled by the investor. However, the investor does have an obligation to keep the broker informed on the status of every open order because the exchange specialist must receive confirmation at regular intervals. Many brokerage firms do not accept stop orders or GTC orders for unlisted stocks.

Year	Annual Price Range	Shares Bought	Shares Owned at Year End	Average Price	Estimated Annual Dividend
1967	$62⅝ - 46¾	36	36	$55½	$ 25
1968	54⅜ - 41⅝	42	78	51¼	68
1969	56 - 42⅞	41	119	50⅜	118
1970	49⅜ - 31⅜	54	173	46⅛	175
1971	46⅝ - 24	58	231	43¼	242
1972	38⅛ - 25⅞	59	290	41⅜	313
1973	53⅝ - 31⅞	49	339	41¼	399
1974	52⅝ - 25⅞	52	391	40⅞	489
1975	50¼ - 27⅛	49	440	40⅞	557
1976	61¼ - 38½	37	477	41⅞	628

Dollar Cost Averaging

There are no magic formulas to stock market investing, but one widely used and frequently successful approach is *dollar cost averaging*. Dollar cost averaging involves purchasing the same dollar amount of stock at regular intervals regardless of price. As a result, more shares are bought at low prices than at high prices. Dollar cost averaging usually works well when the investor:

(1) Has an investment horizon of at least several years.
(2) Selects a high quality stock that, preferably, pays a dividend.
(3) Selects a company that has favorable growth prospects that could lead to a rising stock price over the long term.
(4) Is able to invest a minimum of $1,000 per year (commission costs are quite high otherwise).
(5) Is willing to continue the program relentlessly — barring any substantial change in the company's long term outlook.

As an example of dollar cost averaging, here is the result of a ten-year (1967-1976) investment program involving Aluminum Company of America (Alcoa), the world's leading aluminum producer. Alcoa's stock was a disappointing investment in this specific time frame and was selected for that reason.

During the period, the company's earnings record was erratic. Adjusted for a 1974 stock split, Aloca's profits rose from $3.21 per share in 1966 to $4.14 per share in 1976. At the same time, the dividend was gradually increased from $1.03 per share to $1.37 per share. The stock price in early 1967 was $57 per share and ended 1976 at about the same level.

The table above illustrates the results of investing $500 quarterly throughout the ten year period since 1966. The program was accomplished by buying the rounded number of Alcoa shares $500 would purchase each time. After ten years, the total capital investment was $20,000 before commissions (probably not more than $800).

Dividends obviously become more important as time passes. Had the program been continued, most of the $2,000 annual investment today would be contributed by Alcoa's dividend checks.

The investor successfully reduced the average price per share even though the stock was unchanged during the period. This case illustrates how dollar cost averaging can help a long term investor who fails to select a rising stock. There were, of course, many investments during the same period that produced better and worse results than Alcoa.

Bear Market Strategies

Stock prices will tend to rise over the very long term. They always have. Yet, since World War I, there have been no fewer than ten major bear markets in which stocks declined dramatically. In the stock market crash of 1929-32 and, again, in 1973-74, market values of hundreds of stocks were reduced by more than half. Moreover, as a general rule, prices often drop faster than they rise. Experienced investors know the portfolio "disasters" that occur frequently in bear markets can be devastating to the long term performance of a portfolio. While most people are merely trying to preserve capital in a bear market, the risk-oriented investor regards market weakness as an opportunity to make a substantial profit.

There are several ways to make money in a bear market:

• Buying Contramarket Stocks.
When the market (measured by the averages or any broad list) is advancing or declining, the contramarket stock will be moving in the opposite direction. It is usually among an industry group that has attracted special attention for one reason or another. A contramarket stock is especially noticeable during a bear market when everything else is dropping. Each bear market is different. In years past, the groups that outperformed the market were oil and gas in 1946; pharmaceuticals, food and tobacco in 1957; gold briefly in 1962; and coal and automobile replacement parts in 1969-70. The worst bear market since the 1930's occurred in 1973-74 when gold, sugar, steel and fertilizer stocks were in favor.

Once a bear market has ended, contramarket stocks do not follow a definite pattern. Sometimes they continue rising, sometimes they turn down immediately. In any case, the investor should investigate the company before buying. It is not advisable to buy a stock simply because it is going up when other stocks are declining.

• Buying Put Options.
A put option is a contract to *sell* 100 shares at a definite price within a specified time limit. The put option buyer (who expects the stock price to be going down in the short term) purchases the right to "put" the stock to someone else under the terms of the contract.

There are two primary reasons for buying a put option in a bear market: (1) As a leveraged, high-risk vehicle to obtain a quick capital gain, or (2) As a defensive hedge against a stock the investor does not want to sell for various reasons — usually taxes.

Writing Naked Call Options.

A call option is a contract to *buy* 100 shares at a definite price within a specified time limit. A call option buyer (who expects the stock price to rise in the short term) purchases the right to "call" the stock from someone else under the terms of the contract. Thus, an investor who owns 100 shares of stock and believes its price might be going down, can write a call option against those shares and sell the option to someone who believes the stock price will be going up. Writing a call option when the stock is not owned is referred to as "writing a naked call option." The writer of a naked call option can only profit by the amount received from the option buyer, but much more can be lost. In other words, the writer is a speculator willing to bet the stock will not be rising within the time limit of the contract. Writing a naked call option is, obviously, a high-risk undertaking.

Short Selling.

Selling stock short is the best way for most investors to make money in a bear market. This approach is not appropriate for everyone, however. There is an additional risk involved and the tax bite can be greater.

In effect, the normal sequence of the purchase and sale is reversed. When stock is sold short, the brokerage firm either lends the stock to the customer or borrows it for the customer, who then sells it in the open market. Eventually the same number of shares will have to be repurchased (referred to as "short covering") and be returned to the lender. If the repurchase price is lower because the stock dropped as expected, the short seller will make a profit. If the price is higher, more money will be needed to cover the same number of shares and the short seller will suffer a loss.

There is a special risk to short selling. Stock that is bought "long" in the regular way cannot drop below zero and, therefore, does not involve a loss greater than the total investment. But a stock sold short could, theoretically, produce unlimited losses. There is no ceiling to a stock's appreciation potential. For this reason, the fear of being "squeezed" can make the short seller a more restless investor. To limit this potential loss, the short seller can use a stop order or purchase a call option as a hedge against the short position.

Step 1.

$$\text{Current Margin} = \frac{\text{Proceeds} + \text{Deposit}}{\text{Market Value}} - 1.000$$

Step 2.

$$\text{Current Equity} = \text{Current Margin} \ X \ \text{Market Value}$$

Unless the investor is experienced with short selling, it is best *not* to short a stock that (1) has a favorable fundamental outlook (i.e., having earnings gains or an improving profit trend); (2) has already suffered a price decline of 60% or more; (3) has been strong technically (e.g., the price should not be above its average price of the prior 200 days) or (4) is a candidate for a merger.

In the discussion of margin earlier, short selling was not explained to avoid confusion. It is more complicated . A short seller must know three things to calculate the current equity figure in the margin account:

(1) The initial credit (deposit).

(2) The stock's current market value.

(3) The net proceeds of the short sale.

Current equity can be found by using the two-step formula shown above.

As an example, assume an investor sells short 100 shares of Baltimore Buggy Whip at $70 after depositing $5,000 cash into the margin account. The formula would read:

$$.714 = \frac{\$7,000 + \$5,000}{\$7,000} - 1.000$$

$$\$5,000 = .714 \ X \ \$7,000$$

If the stock declines to $55, the short sale becomes profitable and current equity increases:

$$1.182 = \frac{\$7,000 + \$5,000}{\$5,500} - 1.000$$

$$\$6,500 = 1.182 \ X \ \$5,500$$

On the other hand, if Baltimore Buggy Whip had advanced to $85, the short seller's equity would have been reduced:

$$.412 = \frac{\$7,000 + \$5,000}{\$8,500} - 1.000$$

$$\$3,500 = .412 \ X \ \$8,500$$

As the stock rises, the current margin drops which, in turn, reduces current equity. At $85 and a current margin of 41%, the investor is probably unhappy, but still safe from a margin call. If the brokerage firm's maintenance requirement happens to be 35% on short sale transactions, a margin call for an additional deposit would be issued if the stock advances to $89.

Taxes

Tax laws are complicated. To make matters worse, they are always changing. When tax problems are encountered, it is advisable to seek the help of an accountant. In fact, a few of the strategies suggested in this book will require tax guidance.

Active investors are constantly faced with tax decisions. The tax rate is lower on a long term profit than it is on a short term profit. Should the stock be held a few months longer for a lower tax rate or should the profit be taken now? Capital losses can be very important. Should they be taken now? If not now, when? These are questions investors must answer.

The Tax Reform Act of 1976 presented several tax law changes for investors. Included was a change in the "capital gains holding period." Until December 31, 1976, the length of time an investor must hold a stock to qualify as a long term capital gain or loss was "more than six months." In 1977, the holding period was extended to "more than nine months" and beginning January 1, 1978, the holding period became "more than twelve months." Another important change, among others, was the amount of net capital losses which may be offset against ordinary income in any year. Prior to 1977, a net capital loss could offset up to $1,000 of ordinary income. The new law

increased this amount to $2,000 in 1977 and $3,000 beginning in 1978. Any capital losses in excess of these amounts must be carried forward to future years.

If an individual would like to continue investing in the stock market and wants to establish a tax loss, there are basically three things that can be done:

(1) Sell the stock outright and repurchase it 31 days or more later.

(2) Purchase an equal number of shares (called "doubling-up") and sell the original holdings 31 days later.

(3) Sell the stock and immediately replace it with another stock.

Investors who want to postpone profits from one year to the next can use a technique called "shorting against the box." This transaction is essentially the same as normal short selling except the short position is covered by similar shares already in the account rather than borrowing stock from the broker.

Investors should avoid waiting until late December to work out a tax strategy. The thought process should continue throughout the year. Investors should remember also — to qualify for gains that year, stocks must be sold at least five business days (not including holidays) before year end.

Arbitrage

On Wall Street, the term "arbitrage" refers to the simultaneous purchase and sale of two different securities which have a close relationship (e.g., a convertibility of one security into the other) to take advantage of a disparity in their prices. This activity can apply to equivalent securities trading in different markets, or securities with convertible features, or securities involved in mergers, tender offers, recapitalizations or corporate divestitures.

A "merger arbitrageur," sometimes known as the riverboat gambler of Wall Street, will risk a substantial loss in an attempt to make a small, quick profit. The purchase of one stock and short selling the other eliminates all risk except a change in the agreement that reduces the terms of the merger — an unusual situation — or a termination of the proposal — a much more likely possibility. In other words, if the proposed merger is completed, a smart merger arbitrageur will almost always make a profit. If the marriage is not consumated, however, the purchased stock could decline sharply and the short stock could rise, producing a substantial loss.

Hundreds of viable arbitrage opportunities arise each year (the record number of mergers and acquisitions in a single year is 6,107 in 1969).

There are several brokerage firms that specialize in arbitrage activity and make a point of being well-informed. The spreads, therefore, tend to be fairly representative of the risk involved.

An individual willing to assume the risks of merger arbitrage should establish a list of personal criteria and concentrate on only the mergers that meet those standards. For example, it might be advisable for the acquired company to be high quality, medium-sized, and in a growing field that is different from the acquiring company. As such, there could easily be other suitors and the chance of government intervention would be less.

Because the risks in merger arbitrage are obviously high, the investor should either make an effort to become knowledgeable about the companies involved, or avoid merger arbitrage altogether.

Investment Clubs An individual seeking fun, education and profit can join or start an investment club. Typically, it is a group of 10 to 15 friends who meet once a month to manage their collective investment portfolio. The monthly contribution from each member, a modest sum that is convenient to the membership, is pooled and usually invested in growth stocks using a dollar cost averaging approach. Dividends and capital gains are reinvested in most cases.

There are about 7,000 investment clubs in the U.S. today. Many of these clubs belong to the National Association of Investment Clubs (NAIC), a non-profit organization that provides guidance and literature to its membership. Individuals may be NAIC members for a $15 annual fee or clubs may belong for an annual payment of $20 plus $3 per member. Further information on investment clubs or on the NAIC may bo ob tained by writing:

The National Association
of Investment Clubs
1515 E. Eleven Mile Road
Royal Oak, Michigan 48067

Investment Companies Being part owner of a portfolio that is managed by professionals is a good alternative for individuals who:

(1) Neither have interest in security analysis nor time for their own portfolios;

(2) Do not want to pay an investment advisor;

(3) Are willing to give up some capital appreciation to obtain portfolio diversification.

There are two kinds of funds that investment companies manage: *open-end funds,* also called *mutual funds,* and *closed-end funds.* An open-end fund deals directly with investors and always stands ready to sell or buy its shares at current net asset value. Stated differently, an investor can buy shares from an open-end fund (subscribe) or sell shares to the fund (redeem) at any time. As a result, money flows in or out of a mutual fund when investors subscribe for or redeem shares. A closed-end fund, on the other hand, has a fixed number of charoo outotanding and investors buy or sell them in the open market like any other stock. Because the market price rises or falls according to supply and demand, the price of a closed-end fund share can be at a premium or, most likely, at a discount to its net asset value at any time. Therefore, if the investor wants the market value of each share to directly reflect the net asset value of the fund's portfolio, an open-end fund is preferable to a closed-end fund.

A mutual fund can be either a "load fund" or a "no-load fund." When an investor buys a load fund, a sales charge (called the "load") is immediately deducted from the investment to compensate the salesman who sold the fund. This fee is typically 8% or more. However, a no-load fund is bought directly from the investment company, and the investor is not charged a fee. Otherwise, load funds and no-load funds are comparable in terms of their operations and investment performances.

The names and addresses of many mutual funds can be obtained by sending a stamped, self-addressed envelope with the request to these addresses:

The Investment Company Institute
1775 K Street Northwest
Washington, D.C. 20006

or

No-Load Mutual Fund Association
Valley Forge, PA 19481

Unless there is a strong reason to prefer a particular load fund management, no-load funds should be considered first. A load fund portfolio must grow annually about 2% faster than a no-load fund portfolio for investors in each just to be even at the end of a five year period.

There are five basic types of mutual funds:

- *Common Stock Funds* invest almost entirely in equities (common stocks), although their objectives vary considerably. *Growth funds* are seeking capital appreciation by selecting companies that should grow more rapidly than the general economy. *Aggressive growth funds* buy shares in small or more speculative growth companies for maximum capital appreciation. *Growth/income funds* seek long term capital appreciation with income, and *special purpose funds* attempt to satisfy certain investment interests such as participation in gold or energy. *Index funds,* the newest type, buy representative stocks simply to do no worse than the market indices.

- *Income Funds* are portfolios consisting of bonds and common stocks as well as preferred stocks. Income fund managers try to obtain satisfactory interest and dividend income for the shareholders.

- *Bond Funds* seek high income and preservation of capital by investing primarily in bonds and selecting the proper mix between short term, intermediate term and long term bond maturities. In recent years, tax-free *municipal bond funds* have been popular.

- *Balanced Funds* buy both common stocks and bonds based on a popular belief that conditions unfavorable to common stocks are oftentimes favorable to bonds and vice versa.

- *Money Market Funds* offer their shareholders a means of participating in the high quality, short term instruments of the money market including certificates of deposit, treasury bills and commercial paper.

As a general rule, the larger the fund, the less capital appreciation one should expect relative to the market. Conversely, a small fund requires extreme caution. For most investors' needs, the optimum size of a common stock fund is $50 million to $500 million.

The challenge to the mutual fund investor is selecting an investment company capable of superior performance taking into consideration the fund's investment objectives.

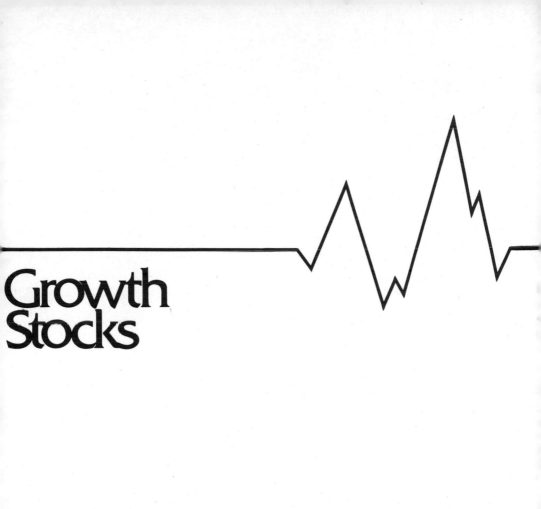

Growth
Stocks

Introduction The "Growth Stock Theory" of investing is not new; it can be traced at least back to the 1930's. Simply stated, this investment concept involves the purchase of shares in companies that, over the years, increase earnings and dividends faster than the growth rate of the general economy. A true growth company has some control over its own destiny because it has the ability to finance itself internally by reinvesting earnings back into the business.

Growth stocks, appropriate for many but not all portfolios, require patience and usually possess somewhat higher market risk initially due to their higher price/earnings ratios. But if the investor knows how to select and value them, growth stocks can provide excellent protection against the ever-increasing cost of living.

This chapter further defines the Growth Stock Theory, shows how companies grow and, most importantly, helps investors identify growth stocks and determine how much to pay for them.

Why a Growth Stock? The power of compounding values, frequently overlooked and usually underestimated, is brought to light by growth stock investing. A company that grows at a compound rate of 15% per year, for example, doubles in size in five years, triples in eight years, and grows to ten times its original size in seventeen years.

How does the growth stock investor benefit? Here is a highly simplified explanation...

Assume:

A growth company earning $1.00 per share today increases its earnings at an average growth rate of 15% per year for twelve years.

Each year the company pays out 30% of earnings as a cash dividend to its stockholders.

The price/earnings ratio of the stock today is twenty times earnings.

The price/earnings ratio in the twelfth year is fifteen times earnings (a lower P/E ratio reflects the probability of a slower growth rate in later years).

	Today	Year Twelve
Earnings Per Share	$1.00	$5.35
Dividend Per Share	$0.30	$1.60
P/E Ratio	20 times	15 times
Stock Price	$20.00	$80.25
Current Dividend Yield	1.5%	2.0%
Dividend Yield on Original Investment	1.5%	8.0%

The buyer of 100 shares today would be investing $2,000. The initial $30 dividend from the company, representing a yield of only 1.5%, is small compared with the higher returns other investments offer.

But by the twelfth year, the market value of the 100 shares becomes $8,025 and more than $800 in dividends has been received over the years. The twelfth year dividend check, $160, is not 1.5% but now 8% of the original investment! If the company continues to grow beyond the twelfth year and the dividend is further increased in line with earnings, the annual return becomes even greater.

It is not uncommon for a long term growth stock investor to be receiving a large return on the original investment in the form of an annual dividend check. An investor in IBM in 1953, for example, receives a dividend today larger than the entire original investment. This is the power of compounding values and the advantage of growth stocks.

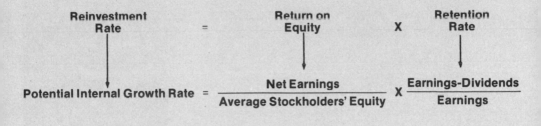

Measuring Growth For a growth company to be successful, it must earn a high return on stockholders' equity and a significant portion of that return must be reinvested into the business. In the calculations to follow, "return on equity" is based on the average of a given year's beginning and ending stockholders' equity. Many successful growth companies such as Baxter Laboratories and Hewlett-Packard have increased their growth rates through the skillful addition of outside capital. But the ability to grow internally is crucial in the long run.

A company's internal growth rate potential is best measured by the "reinvestment rate" formula illustrated above.

For example, if a company has a return on average equity of 16%, earns $4.00 per share and pays an annual dividend of $1.00 per share, the reinvestment rate would be calculated in this manner:

In other words, unless this company improves its return on equity or pays out proportionately less to stockholders, it could not grow faster than 12% per year without assuming additional debt or selling new stock.

As valuable as it is, the reinvestment rate formula should be used with care. A low-quality company can attain a high return on equity if stockholders' equity is small in relation to profits (perhaps the result of many unprofitable years). When a company's return on equity and return on assets are both high, the reinvestment rate formula can be used with greater confidence.

Growth rate calculations, profitability measurements and other analytical techniques become especially useful when companies operating in the same industry or with similar characteristics are compared with one another.

Reinvestment Rate		Return on Equity	X	Retention Rate
Potential Internal Growth Rate	=	16%	X	$\dfrac{\$4.00-\$1.00}{\$4.00}$
12%	=	16%	X	75%

110

Learning from the Past As the following examples indicate, growth stock investing can produce favorable results if the investor is patient, owns the right stocks and does not pay excessive prices. In 1950, Eastman Kodak, Minnesota Mining & Manufacturing and Procter & Gamble were already recognized growth companies. A $1,000 investment in each of these growth stocks that year would have produced the following results twenty-five years later without the benefit of reinvesting dividends.

	Cost	Market Value on 12/31/75	Cash Dividend Received in 1975
Eastman Kodak	$1,000	$17,688	$343
3M	$1,000	$18,500	$450
Procter & Gamble	$1,000	$10,471	$235
TOTAL	**$3,000**	**$46,659**	**$1,028**

What will be the value of this portfolio in the year 2000? No one can say for sure, but if the earnings and dividends of these three companies continue to grow at healthy rates, the portfolio value will probably be considerably higher. Obviously, their growth rates will slow as they get larger. Yet, at a rate of only 7% per year, the combined annual cash dividends alone will total $5,579 in the year 2000.

An investor compiling a list of top growth companies having capable managements, attractive product opportunities and a return on equity exceeding 12% in 1963 surely would have included most, if not all, of the well-known companies listed in Table I. The figures are presented as they appeared that year and as they appeared twelve years later as shown in Table II. Assuming $1,000 was invested in each of these companies in 1963 (at the highest prices of the year to allow for unfortunate timing), this $10,000 portfolio would have been valued at $28,377 twelve years later, as seen in Table III, despite the sharp contraction of P/E multiples during this period. In addition, the cash dividends received from this portfolio in 1975 would have totaled $516 or 5.2% of the original investment. Again, these results exclude the benefit of dividend reinvestment.

In the years since 1975, the overall portfolio value has been both higher and lower. Yet, as a group, these companies have continued to grow. The need for patience is clear, but how does one select the right stocks and know how much to pay for them?

George Eastman (1854-1932) performed early photographic experiments in his mother's kitchen. In 1881, he and a family friend established the Eastman Dry Plate Company, later known as Eastman Kodak Company.

Table I 10 Recognized Growth Stocks

	— $MM — Sales	Working Capital	Operating Margin %	Earnings Per Share	Dividend Per Share	Reinvest-ment Rate %	1963 Price Range	Median P/E Ratio	Shares Outstanding (000)
American Home Products	$532	$105	22.1%	$2.45	$1.60	9.6%	$65¾-$49⅜	23.5	23,252
Avon Products	249	51	21.6	3.08	1.90	14.1	135½-87½	36.2	9,558
Bristol Myers	232	46	15.8	1.81	0.90	10.7	62⅝-43	29.2	10,480
Caterpillar Tractor	966	292	16.5	2.83	1.15	11.2	49⅝-34⅝	14.9	27,294
Hewlett-Packard	116	34	12.1	0.60	nil	14.4	27¼-18½	38.1	11,212
Int'l. Business Machines	2,060	777	26.4	10.45	4.25	11.6	509⅜-384¼	42.8	27,793
Kellogg Co.	322	45	14.3	1.56	0.85	10.2	44¾-27½	23.2	17,918
Polaroid Corp.	122	52	18.9	2.84	0.20	13.9	211½-120½	58.5	3,935
Texas Instruments	277	55	9.0	2.41	0.64	9.5	77⅞-45⅝	25.6	4,994
Xerox Corp.	176	17	30.7	1.13	0.20	28.4	86⅞-29¼	51.4	20,340

Thomas A. Edison (1847-1931) said: "Genius is two percent inspiration and ninety-eight percent perspiration." The Edison General Electric Company, founded in 1878, was a predecessor to the General Electric Company.

Table II — 10 Recognized Growth Stocks Twelve Years Later

	— $ MM —								
	Sales	Working Capital	Operating Margin %	Earnings Per Share	Dividend Per Share	Reinvestment Rate %	12/31/75 Price	Median P/E Ratio	Shares Outstanding (000)
American Home Products	$2,409	$ 628	25.8%	$1.58	$0.90	12.5%	$33⅜	22.5	156,985
Avon Products	1,295	339	21.7	2.40	1.51	10.3	34⅞	16.5	58,028
Bristol Myers	1,828	499	14.6	4.44	1.58	14.0	69	13.5	31,365
Caterpillar Tractor	4,964	1,108	22.3	6.97	1.85	18.2	69¾	8.9	57,285
Hewlett-Packard	981	320	14.5	3.02	0.25	15.0	94½	29.3	27,751
Int'l. Business Machines	14,437	4,752	23.7	13.35	6.50	9.5	224¼	14.4	149,854
Kellogg Co.	1,214	198	16.9	1.40	0.72	13.2	21½	13.3	73,632
Polaroid Corp.	813	486	13.3	1.91	0.32	7.8	31	15.3	32,855
Texas Instruments	1,368	361	8.4	2.71	1.00	6.9	94¾	22.3	22,925
Xerox Corp	4,054	571	22.1	4.29	1.00	14.3	50⅞	15.6	79,194

Table III — Portfolio Results

	% Increase EPS 1963-75	100 Shares in 1963 Becomes:	# Shares Purch. in 1963	# Shares Held in 1975	Value of $1000 on 12/31/75	Dividends in 1975
Amer. Home Prod.	+285%	600 shares	15.2	91.2	$ 3,044	$ 82
Avon Products	+371	600	7.3	43.8	1,528	66
Bristol Myers	+390	200	16.0	32.0	2,208	51
Caterpillar Tractor	+389	200	20.2	40.4	2,818	75
Hewlett-Packard	+907	200	36.7	73.4	6,936	18
IBM	+391	480	2.0	9.6	2,153	62
Kellogg Co.	+259	400	22.3	89.2	1,918	64
Polaroid Corp.	+431	800	4.7	37.6	1,166	12
Texas Instruments	+352	400	12.8	51.2	4,851	51
Xerox Corp.	+1,029	300	11.5	34.5	1,755	35
					$28,377	$516

Below is a case study of two companies operating in the same industry at the same time to illustrate the thought process. It is especially important for the investor to see the *big picture* and watch the "two P's" of growth stock investing ... Profitability and Progress. An improving trend in profitability can help investment performance markedly.

Air Products was much more aggressive than Airco in its pursuit of growth in the 1960's. The importance of both internal and external financing is very obvious in this case.

Air Products amplified the impact of its improving profitability and high earnings retention with additional debt to finance long term gas sales contracts. This strategy produced superior growth for Air Products in the 1965-75 period. As a result, Air Products' stockholders enjoyed better investment performance. This thought process must be repeated periodically because past trends can change at any time.

— Air Products vs. Airco Inc. —

AIRCO INC.
(formerly Air Reduction Co.)

	Sales	Operating Margin %	Net Income	Long Term Debt	Return on Equity	Earnings Per Share	Avg. 10-Year EPS Growth	Dividend Per Share
1965	$376.8mm	12.8%	$25.7mm	$124.6mm	12.6%	$2.50	4.5%	$1.25
1975	$765.7mm	12.1%	$42.7mm	$187.7mm	14.0%	$3.76	4.2%	$0.95

Ten Year (1965-75) Investment Performance — 25%

AIR PRODUCTS & CHEMICALS

	Sales	Operating Margin %	Net Income	Long Term Debt	Return on Equity	Earnings Per Share	Avg. 10-Year EPS Growth	Dividend Per Share
1965	$121.1mm	13.7%	$ 7.4mm	$ 94.0mm	11.0%	$0.70	12.4%	$0.04
1975	$699.0mm	17.0%	$54.2mm	$184.1mm	19.7%	$4.02	19.1%	$0.20

Ten Year (1965-75) Investment Performance +328%

NOTE: Per share figures have been adjusted for splits and stock dividends for comparability.

Alexander Graham Bell (1847-1922) is shown (center) in 1906 with the men who strung the first telephone line. Bell Telephone Company, founded in 1877, later became American Telephone & Telegraph Company.

These exercises and other past experiences show that successful growth companies have several characteristics in common. The growth stock investor should, therefore, be looking for a company that has:

- A product or service in good customer demand and profitable enough to finance most or all future growth internally (i.e., capable of a high reinvestment rate).

- A stable or improving trend in profitability and prospects for a better reinvestment rate.

- A capable, imaginative management team that can turn promise into reality.

In addition, there are other related factors to consider. Does the company also have:

- A growth record over the past 5-10 years?

- A solid balance sheet with little debt or the management talent to use debt skillfully?

- Strong marketing and service capabilities?

- An ability to add new or improved products to the current line?

- A position in the marketplace that allows some product pricing flexibility?

- Good labor relations?

At What Price? "What is a share of this company worth?" is the most difficult of all Wall Street questions. A precise answer cannot be found; it is simply a matter of careful analysis and judgment.

In the short term . . . a period of days, weeks or months . . . the price of a stock fluctuates around a consensus of value based on earnings and dividends expectations. This consensus can change gradually or almost immediately. Over the long term . . . a few years or more . . . the stock price will most likely rise or fall in line with the company's actual earnings, dividends and financial condition. This is especially true for growth stocks.

Valuing stocks is extremely complicated because investors always have alternative investment opportunities. Bonds, money market instruments, savings accounts, real estate, art, or personal business ventures are among many examples.

Stock Yields vs. Bond Yields*

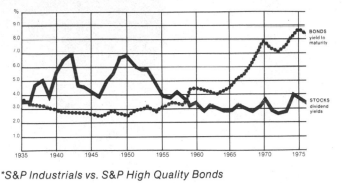

*S&P Industrials vs. S&P High Quality Bonds

Therefore, an investor should make a value decision at three levels:

(1) The investment environment (i.e., the potential return that all stocks offer vs. alternative investment opportunities).

(2) The value of the stock relative to other stocks.

(3) The value of the stock based on its individual merits.

Changes in the investment environment influence P/E ratios and dividend yields of virtually all stocks. Consequently, the investor should keep abreast of factors that might cause change — the two most important being inflation and interest rates.

In the forty years since 1935, there has been a steady decline in the purchasing power of the dollar. Most dramatic during this time were periods of accelerated inflation in 1946-47 and, again, in 1973-74. Interest rates, as measured by the prime rate charged by banks, remained at a low 2-3% level from 1935 until 1951, climbed gradually through the 1950's to about 5%, and maintained that level until about 1966. Since then, the prime rate has risen and fallen sharply, reaching peaks of 8-9% in 1969-70, 12% in 1974 and even higher since.

The chart above shows how the changing investment environment since the Depression has affected stock and bond yields.

Surprisingly, yields on both stocks and high-quality bonds in the fifty years, 1925-1975, averaged about the same — roughly 4.5%. Between 1925 and 1955 stock yields almost always exceeded bond yields but in the twenty years since 1955, the reverse was true. Many observers attribute the noticeable shift since the 1940's to a change in inflation expectations.

History also shows how a changing investment environment can affect P/E ratios. A typical stock P/E ratio in the late 1940's and early 1950's was 8 to 12 times earnings. Throughout most of the 1960's, 15 to 20 times earnings was considered reasonable. In December, 1979, the P/E ratio of the Dow Jones Industrial Average was below 8 times earnings, well under its 14.4 average for the forty year period.

Growth stocks usually command higher P/E ratios and lower yields than ordinary stocks for understandable reasons. Clearly, two stocks having the same P/E ratio or dividend yield are not equally attractive if one is a growth company and the other is not.

Assuming everything else is equal, the company that grows at a faster rate should command a higher P/E ratio. Throughout history securities analysts and market theoreticians have worked tirelessly to devise formulas to value growth stocks. The well-known financial textbook, *Security Analysis,* co-authored by David L. Dodd, Sidney Cottle, and the late Benjamin Graham, presented a valuation formula based on a seven year time horizon. Their work concluded that a company with no growth deserved, at least, the nominal P/E multiple of 8.5 times earnings while, at the other extreme, a company growing at an annual rate of 20% could be assigned a P/E multiple of 41.5 times earnings. By 1973 or 1974 it became obvious that interest rates have an influence (an inverse relationship) on P/E ratios. So the popular Graham & Dodd P/E formula was revised to read as follows:

$$P/E = \frac{37.5 + 8.8g}{i}$$

g – The expected earnings growth rate for the next 7-10 years.

i – The prevailing interest rate for Aaa bonds.

37.5 and 8.8 – Constant values based on experience.

By using this new formula and applying various growth rate and interest rate combinations to it, one can construct a P/E ratio table for easy reference, as shown on the next page.

To use the table, an investor must first estimate the company's annual earnings growth rate for the next seven to ten years. By crossing this growth rate with the prevailing interest rate on the table, the investor can obtain the same P/E multiple had the formula been used.

This formula has one serious shortcoming that should not be ignored, however. If the prevailing interest rate is 7% and there are two companies growing at the same rate of, say, 12%, both stocks deserve a 20.4 P/E ratio according to the formula and the table. Suppose the first company has a higher return on equity and is, therefore, able to pay a higher dividend to its stockholders. Should both companies be selling at the same 20.4 P/E multiple? Obviously not. Another factor to consider is the reliability of the growth projection which depends on the quality of management, the sophistication of products, the strength of competition, patent protection, the capital intensive nature of the business and so on. Thus, investors using this table to compare stock values should be prepared to make a few adjustments.

Henry Ford (1863-1947), pictured in 1915 with his first automobile, formed the Ford Motor Company in 1903. His work signaled the beginning of an industry that enjoyed substantial growth in the early part of the century.

Price/Earnings Ratios Assuming Different Growth Rates and Interest Rates

Prevailing Interest Rate

	3%	4%	5%	6%	7%	8%	9%	10%	11%	12%	13%	14%	15%
20%	71.2	53.4	42.7	35.6	30.5	26.7	23.7	21.4	19.4	17.8	16.4	15.3	14.2
19%	68.2	51.2	40.9	34.1	29.2	25.6	22.7	20.5	18.6	17.1	15.7	14.6	13.6
18%	65.3	49.0	39.2	32.7	28.0	24.5	21.8	19.6	17.8	16.3	15.1	14.0	13.1
17%	62.4	46.8	37.4	31.2	26.7	23.4	20.8	18.7	17.0	15.6	14.4	13.4	12.5
16%	59.4	44.6	35.7	29.7	25.5	22.3	19.8	17.8	16.2	14.9	13.7	12.7	11.9
15%	56.5	42.4	33.9	28.3	24.2	21.2	18.8	17.0	15.4	14.1	13.0	12.1	11.3
14%	53.6	40.2	32.1	26.8	23.0	20.1	17.9	16.1	14.6	13.4	12.4	11.5	10.7
13%	50.6	38.0	30.4	25.3	21.7	19.0	16.9	15.2	13.8	12.7	11.7	10.9	10.1
12%	47.7	35.8	28.6	23.9	20.4	17.9	15.9	14.3	13.0	11.9	11.0	10.2	9.5
11%	44.8	33.6	26.9	22.4	19.2	16.8	14.9	13.4	12.2	11.2	10.3	9.6	9.0
10%	41.8	31.4	25.1	20.9	17.9	15.7	13.9	12.6	11.4	10.5	9.7	9.0	8.4
9%	38.9	29.2	23.3	19.5	16.7	14.6	13.0	11.7	10.6	9.7	9.0	8.3	7.8
8%	36.0	27.0	21.6	18.0	15.4	13.5	12.0	10.8	9.8	9.0	8.3	7.7	7.2
7%	33.0	24.8	19.8	16.5	14.2	12.4	11.0	9.9	9.0	8.3	7.6	7.1	6.6
6%	30.1	22.6	18.1	15.1	12.9	11.3	10.0	9.0	8.2	7.5	6.9	6.5	6.0
5%	27.2	20.4	16.3	13.6	11.6	10.2	9.1	8.2	7.4	6.8	6.3	5.8	5.4
4%	24.2	18.2	14.5	12.1	10.4	9.1	8.1	7.3	6.6	6.1	5.6	5.2	4.8
3%	21.3	16.0	12.8	10.7	9.1	8.0	7.1	6.4	5.8	5.3	4.9	4.6	4.3

Expected Growth Rate (row labels at left, 20% down to 3%)

Most analysts prefer to use five to ten year periods when studying the stock market or individual growth stocks. As mentioned earlier, Graham & Dodd used seven years. *Here, a twelve-year investment time horizon is recommended.*

Any objective analysis of growth stocks requires a time period long enough to encompass at least one or two full economic business cycles as well as enough time to allow a company to grow. However, the time horizon should also be short enough to allow an investor to estimate the future without too much "blue sky." Thus, ten to twelve years should be a good time-frame.

Further, whether by accident, political contrivance, coincidence or whatever, there has been a very distinct four - year buying cycle to the stock market as measured by the Dow Jones Industrial Average. While this pattern may never again repeat, history clearly shows that, with the exception of only one instance (1930), each fourth year since 1914 was an excellent time to buy stocks:

1914	1930	1946	1962
1918	1934	1950	1966
1922	1938	1954	1970
1926	1942	1958	1974

A period of three full market cycles, or twelve years, seems appropriate since twelve-year periods play an interesting role in U.S. history. It was exactly twelve years between the U.S. entry into World War I (1917) and the beginning of the Great Depression (1929) and the U.S. entry into World War II (1941). Twelve years after the end of World War II (1945-46) was the first significant post-war economic recession (1957-58). Twelve years later there was another recession (1970). It is also worth noting that two of the most severe stock market declines since the Great Depression occurred in 1961-62 and, twelve years later, in 1973-74.

The "12-Year Present Value Method" is used to compare the relative values of stocks over a twelve year period. This approach is based, as the name implies, on the present value of future earnings.

An investor using the 12-Year Present Value Method should also take into account dividends that would be received over the twelve year period.

If "Company A" succeeds in growing at 14% annually over the next twelve years, each $1 of earnings today would become $4.82 in the twelfth year. If another company, "Company B," of similar quality, grows at 11% per year, each $1 of earnings would become $3.50 after twelve years. What is the value of the $4.82 and $3.50 *today,* not twelve years from now? The answer depends, of course, on the annual return the investor is seeking.

By using the 12-Year Present Value Table shown on the next page, it can be seen that the $4.82 (14% growth) has a present value of $1.54 and the $3.50 (11% growth) has a present value of $1.12 when the investor is seeking a 10% annual return. If, for some reason, the investor would rather have a 12% annual return, the present value of Company A's future earnings is $1.24 while Company B's is $0.90.

To show how the 12-Year Present Value method works, consider the actual experience of an investor comparing Johnson & Johnson with Coca Cola Company and the Dow Jones Industrial Average back in 1963 (all figures have been adjusted for stock splits):

Johnson & Johnson
Current (1963) Stock Price: $12
Current (1963) EPS: $0.38
Estimated 1963-75 earnings per share growth rate: 19%
Current (1963) P/E ratio: 31.6 times earnings
Desired investment return: 10% per year

Coca-Cola Company
Current (1963) Stock Price: $28
Current (1963) EPS: $0.96
Estimated 1963-75 earnings per share growth rate: 13%
Current (1963) P/E ratio: 29.2 times earnings
Desired investment return: 10% per year

Dow Jones Industrial Average
Current (1963) DJIA Level: 760
Current (1963) EPS: $41.21
Estimated 1963-75 earnings per share growth rate: 5%
Current (1963) P/E ratio: 18.4 times earnings
Desired investment return: 10% per year

Dr. Edwin H. Land (1909-   ), founder of Polaroid Corporation in 1937, unveiled his instant photographic process before the Optical Society of America in February, 1947.

12-Year Present Value Table

Desired Return

Expected Growth Rate	4%	5%	6%	7%	8%	9%	10%	11%	12%	13%	14%	15%	16%	17%	18%	19%	20%
4%	1.00	0.89	0.80	0.71	0.64	0.57	0.51	0.46	0.41	0.37	0.33	0.30	0.27	0.24	0.22	0.20	0.18
5%	1.13	1.00	0.89	0.80	0.71	0.64	0.57	0.52	0.46	0.42	0.38	0.34	0.30	0.27	0.25	0.22	0.20
6%	1.26	1.12	1.00	0.89	0.80	0.72	0.64	0.57	0.52	0.46	0.42	0.38	0.34	0.31	0.28	0.25	0.23
7%	1.41	1.25	1.12	1.00	0.89	0.80	0.72	0.64	0.58	0.52	0.47	0.42	0.38	0.34	0.31	0.28	0.25
8%	1.58	1.40	1.25	1.12	1.00	0.90	0.80	0.72	0.65	0.58	0.52	0.47	0.43	0.38	0.35	0.31	0.28
9%	1.76	1.57	1.40	1.25	1.12	1.00	0.90	0.80	0.72	0.65	0.58	0.53	0.48	0.43	0.38	0.35	0.31
10%	1.96	1.75	1.56	1.39	1.25	1.12	1.00	0.90	0.81	0.73	0.65	0.59	0.53	0.48	0.43	0.39	0.35
11%	2.19	1.95	1.74	1.55	1.39	1.25	1.12	1.00	0.90	0.81	0.73	0.65	0.59	0.53	0.48	0.43	0.39
12%	2.44	2.17	1.94	1.73	1.55	1.39	1.24	1.12	1.00	0.90	0.81	0.73	0.66	0.59	0.53	0.48	0.44
13%	2.71	2.41	2.15	1.92	1.72	1.54	1.38	1.24	1.12	1.00	0.90	0.81	0.73	0.66	0.59	0.54	0.48
14%	3.01	2.68	2.40	2.14	1.91	1.72	1.54	1.37	1.24	1.11	1.00	0.90	0.81	0.73	0.66	0.60	0.54
15%	3.34	2.98	2.66	2.38	2.12	1.90	1.71	1.53	1.37	1.24	1.11	1.00	0.90	0.81	0.73	0.66	0.60
16%	3.71	3.31	2.95	2.64	2.36	2.11	1.89	1.70	1.53	1.37	1.24	1.11	1.00	0.90	0.81	0.74	0.67
17%	4.11	3.67	3.27	2.92	2.61	2.34	2.10	1.88	1.69	1.52	1.37	1.23	1.11	1.00	0.90	0.82	0.74
18%	4.56	4.06	3.62	3.24	2.89	2.60	2.33	2.08	1.87	1.68	1.52	1.36	1.23	1.11	1.00	0.90	0.82
19%	5.04	4.49	4.01	3.58	3.20	2.87	2.57	2.31	2.07	1.86	1.68	1.51	1.36	1.23	1.10	1.00	0.90
20%	5.58	4.97	4.43	3.96	3.54	3.18	2.85	2.55	2.29	2.06	1.85	1.67	1.51	1.36	1.22	1.10	1.00
21%	6.16	5.49	4.90	4.37	3.91	3.51	3.14	2.82	2.53	2.28	2.05	1.84	1.66	1.50	1.35	1.22	1.10
22%	6.79	6.05	5.40	4.83	4.32	3.87	3.47	3.11	2.79	2.51	2.26	2.03	1.83	1.65	1.49	1.35	1.22
23%	7.49	6.68	5.96	5.32	4.76	4.27	3.82	3.43	3.08	2.77	2.49	2.24	2.02	1.82	1.64	1.49	1.34
24%	8.26	7.36	6.56	5.87	5.24	4.70	4.21	3.78	3.39	3.05	2.75	2.47	2.22	2.01	1.81	1.64	1.48
25%	9.09	8.10	7.23	6.46	5.78	5.18	4.64	4.16	3.74	3.36	3.02	2.72	2.44	2.21	1.99	1.80	1.63
26%	10.01	8.92	7.96	7.11	6.36	5.70	5.11	4.58	4.11	3.70	3.33	2.99	2.69	2.43	2.19	1.98	1.79
27%	11.01	9.81	8.75	7.82	6.99	6.27	5.62	5.04	4.53	4.07	3.66	3.29	2.96	2.68	2.41	2.18	1.97
28%	12.09	10.77	9.61	8.59	7.68	6.89	6.17	5.53	4.97	4.47	4.02	3.62	3.25	2.94	2.65	2.40	2.17
29%	13.28	11.83	10.56	9.43	8.43	7.56	6.78	6.07	5.46	4.91	4.42	3.97	3.57	3.23	2.91	2.63	2.38
30%	14.56	12.98	11.58	10.35	9.25	8.29	7.43	6.66	5.99	5.38	4.85	4.36	3.91	3.54	3.19	2.89	2.61

The present value of future earnings for each can be found by simply multiplying the current (1963) earnings per share by the appropriate figures found on the 12-Year Present Value Table (Johnson & Johnson $0.38 × 2.57; Coca-Cola $0.96 × 1.38 and DJIA $41.21 × .57). From these figures, an investor could have calculated P/E multiples based on the present value of future earnings rather than current 1963 earnings. The results proved interesting:

Johnson & Johnson	12.2 times PV earnings
Coca-Cola	21.2 times PV earnings
Dow Jones Industrials	32.4 times PV earnings

Using this method of comparison, in 1963, Coca-Cola was more attractive than the Dow Jones Industrials, not less attractive as implied by the current P/E ratios. Furthermore, Johnson & Johnson appeared to be considerably more attractive than both Coca-Cola and the DJIA as the stock price performances subsequently proved.

Johnson & Johnson	1963-75 stock performance: **+650%**
Coca-Cola	1963-75 stock performance: **+207%**
DJIA	1963-75 stock performance: **+13%**

Investors can use the Table to compare today's investment values by performing the same calculations with current earnings per share figures. However, the key to successful growth stock investing is good fundamental research and a correct analysis of earnings growth potential. Without the proper input, these and other formulas are practically useless.

Other Methods When Benjamin Graham, known as the Dean of security analysts, was asked for his approach to common stocks, he offered several suggestions. He looked for a common stock selling at less than its working capital (net current asset value), giving no weight to a company's plant and other fixed assets — although he did realize this approach would be limited. He also favored other conservative valuation methods such as: (1) Paying no more than 7 times reported earnings of the past twelve months, (2) Requiring a current dividend yield of at least 7% and, (3) Preferring companies with a book value greater than 120% of the stock price. Unfortunately, growth stocks are rarely available at such attractive levels because investors also place a value on future earnings prospects.

Perspective Growth stock investors should be especially wary of "investment fads." An industry will sometimes flourish for only one or two years allowing its participants to resemble true growth companies. Examples, among many others, include boating in the late 1950's, bowling and certain electronics businesses in the early 1960's, conglomerates and computer leasing in the late 1960's and warehouse merchandising in the early 1970's.

An investor can avoid being deceived by correctly identifying the strengths and weaknesses of the industry, understanding the economics of the business, and maintaining long term perspective. Common sense is the growth stock investor's most valuable tool.

For a closer look at growth stock investing, one book especially recommended is *Finding the Next Super Stock* ($6.95) by "Wall Street Week" panelist Frank A. Cappiello. (Published by Liberty Publishing Company, Inc., 1982).

Bonds, preferred stocks and the money market

Introduction Sophisticated investors tailor
their investment portfolios to meet their
individual financial needs. They realize,
too, that an individual's needs change with
time; that an elderly widow has a different
financial objective than a young business
executive just starting a family.

Many investors find they require more
current income and greater safety of principal than can be expected of a portfolio
invested entirely in common stocks. This
chapter will explain several alternatives
including bonds, preferred stocks and
issues of the United States Government. It
will also touch on the meaning and content
of the "money market" where short-term
credit instruments and negotiable paper
are traded.

Bond trading has changed since the early 1900's

Bonds Explained News commentators frequently conclude their daily reports with a description of the day's stock market activity, but there is seldom, if ever, any mention of bonds. Widely regarded as the most conservative investment, bonds generally do not experience the dramatic day-to-day price changes that make for exciting reporting. Yet, the bond market is several times larger than the stock market. In recent years roughly 80% of all new corporate financing has been accomplished through bonds. Further, it has been estimated that nearly as many individuals own bonds as own common stocks.

Bonds are issued (sold) by corporations, state and local governments or their agencies, the United States government, foreign governments and Federal agencies. Professional bond traders use one word designations for the bonds of each issue which are, respectively: corporates, municipals, governments and agencies.

Although each type of bond has certain unique characteristics, bonds in general have one basic function — they are formal IOU's in which the issuer promises to repay the total amount borrowed on a predetermined date. In addition, for the use of the money, the issuer will also compensate the bondholder with, typically, semi-annual interest payments at a fixed per-

centage rate during each year the bond is owned. In the language of bonds, the total amount to be repaid is called variously its "principal amount" or "face value" or "par value;" the repayment date is known as the "maturity date;" the interest rate is the bond's "coupon" and the period of time the bond is outstanding is called its "term." All this information is printed on the face of the bond.

In the past, nearly all bond certificates came with coupons attached. The coupons were periodically clipped from the bond and presented for payment. This is, in fact, the derivation of the term "coupon" which became synonymous with fixed interest payment. Bonds can be issued in "registered" form (the owner's name is registered with the corporation and interest payments are mailed directly to the bondholder) and "bearer" form (the bond is presumed to belong to whoever possesses it). Most corporates are registered bonds while municipals, on the other hand, are still issued as bearer bonds.

A bond certificate, then, is a certificate of indebtedness spelling out terms of the issuer's promise to repay. Sometimes, this promise is reinforced by collateral such as equipment or property, but usually bonds offer only the "full faith and credit" of the borrower (bonds of this type are called

Bonds	Cur Yld	Vol	High	Low	Close	Net Chg
Exxon 6½98	7.6	43	86	85	85	− ⅞
ExP 8.05s80	7.8	8	103¼	103¼	103¼	.....
ExP 7.65s83	7.7	57	100	100	100	− ¼
FMC 4¼92	cv	31	72½	72	72	−1
Fairch 4⅜92	cv	60	60	59⅛	60	.....

debentures). For this reason, obligations issued by the U.S. government are regarded as the safest investments available.

A corporate certificate of indebtedness contrasts sharply with a common stock certificate which signifies ownership. If the company prospers, its common stockholders can expect to share in the expanding profits through a combination of dividend increases and a higher stock price. The bondholder cannot share in the company's growth and can only expect repayment of the principal amount and the fixed annual interest payments. If the company fails, however, the bondholders and owners of preferred stock, which resemble bonds in many ways, must be paid in full before the common stockholders get a cent. For this reason, bonds and preferred stock are known as "senior securities."

Bonds are issued with various face values or "denominations" ... usually set at $1,000 a bond. When the bond trades in the open market, however, its price is quoted at 1/10th of its value. Thus, a bond selling at par, or $1,000, would be listed as 100; a bond selling above par or, in other words, at a "premium," say $1,100, would be shown as 110. A bond trading below par or at a "discount," say $880, would appear as 88. Bonds, like stocks, also trade at fractional prices in increments of eighths.

Thus, a bond priced at 88⅛ corresponds to a dollar value of $881.25. A bond at 105⅞ is the same as $1,058.75.

Government bonds are traded in a similar fashion but their fractions are expressed in thirty-seconds. A government bond selling for 90.12 means $90^{12}/_{32}$ which reduces to 90⅜ or a dollar equivalent of $903.75.

Shown above is a typical excerpt from the New York Exchange corporate bond table that appears daily in the *Wall Street Journal* and other newspapers.

Consider the bond of Exxon Corporation, a well-known oil company, as an example. Reading from left to right, the investor learns that the bond was issued by Exxon, pays an annual interest rate of 6½ per cent, matures in 1998 and, on this particular day, carried a "current yield" of 7.6 per cent, which will be explained shortly. The remaining figures describe that day's trading. They tell the reader that $43,000 of this specific issue traded that day at prices as high as 86 or $860 and as low as 85 or $850. The final trade of the day took place at 85 which was ⅞ths of a point ($8.75) lower than the final price recorded in the preceding trading session.

The investor may wonder why bond prices fluctuate at all since the bondholder has been promised full repayment at maturity. This question can best be answered within

An interest rate can be regarded as the purchase price of money.

the larger context of interest rates — the key to understanding bonds.

An interest rate can be regarded as the purchase price of money. Basically when there is high demand for money by business, consumers, and governments, and the supply is limited as it is during a period of economic expansion, the cost of money (expressed by the interest rate) rises. When demand is slack and money is freely available, as it is during an economic slowdown or recession, the interest rate falls.

There is no single interest rate, but several. These include the *Prime rate,* the interest rate that banks charge their most credit-worthy borrowers; the *Federal Funds rate,* the interest rate charged on loans made between banks that are members of the Federal Reserve System; the *Federal Reserve Discount rate* that member banks pay on funds borrowed from their Federal Reserve Bank and *Money Market rates* (including issues of the United States government such as Treasury bills). Although there are frequently differences between the interest rate levels of various issues, all rates tend to move together (note the chart on the next page). At any given time, interest rates reflect not only current conditions, but also investor expectations of future trends.

Yields: New bonds are issued at rates dictated by economic conditions and expectations. As rates change, the return investors expect from bonds already trading in the open market (called "yields") must be adjusted to remain competitive and attractive to investors. Since the annual interest payment is fixed throughout a bond's life, the adjustment must be made through the price of the bond itself.

Like common stocks, a bond's current yield is found by dividing its annual interest payment by its price (with stocks the expected annual dividend is divided by its price). When a bond is bought at par, or face value, its current yield is, obviously, identical to its coupon rate. But, if it is purchased at any other price, its current yield will be more or less than its coupon rate. As the example on the next page illustrates, the yield on a $1,000 par value bond paying $90 can decline or rise in response to a change in the price of the bond. A bond's price and its yield always move in opposite directions.

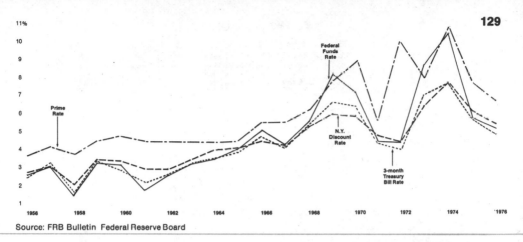

Source: FRB Bulletin Federal Reserve Board

---

(1) When the bond price
is at par:
$$\frac{\$90}{\$1,000} = 9.00\%$$

---

(2) When the bond price
rises, its yield
declines:
$$\frac{\$90}{\$1,100} = 8.18\%$$

---

(3) When the bond price
declines, its yield rises:
$$\frac{\$90}{\$900} = 10.00\%$$

Price, then, is the basic adjustment mechanism which conforms yield to the general level of interest rates. To repeat, even though bondholders receive full face value at maturity, a bond's price will fluctuate during its life for a very simple reason ... if all other factors are equal, an investor would never buy an existing bond from another bondholder when new comparable issues being offered elsewhere are providing higher returns.

While bond prices normally do not swing as widely or as rapidly as common stock prices, potential bond investors should realize that bond prices do fluctuate nevertheless. If a bond must be sold before its maturity date, it is possible that the bondholder will receive less than face value, and perhaps substantially less.

The term "current yield" was adequate to explain why and how bond prices change, but the most important measure of a bond's return to the bondholder is called the "yield to maturity." At par, a bond's yield to maturity equals its current yield and its coupon rate, but if a bond is purchased at a premium or at a discount, its yield to maturity will be either less or more than its current yield. At any price other than par, the yield to maturity differs from and is more accurate than the current yield. It recognizes that, in addition to the annual interest payments received during the life of the bond, the bondholder can also receive a capital gain or loss at maturity if there is a difference between the purchase price and the face value. Yield to maturity computes the compound annual interest gained or lost on this difference, assigns (or more exactly "amortizes") a portion to each year of the bond's remaining life and expresses the result as a single annual percentage rate. In effect, if a bond is purchased at a discount, the yield to maturity is greater than the current yield. If a bond is bought at a premium, the yield to maturity is less than current yield.

Although in practice, a bond's yield to maturity is usually calculated by computers, it can also be approximated by using a bond value table. The bond value table gives the yield to maturity at various maturities, coupons and prices. The yields

6½% **YEARS** and MONTHS

Yield	18-6	19-0	19-6	20-0	20-6	21-0	21-6	22-0
4.00	132.46	133.05	133.63	134.19	134.75	135.29	135.83	136.35
4.20	129.38	129.90	130.41	130.91	131.40	131.88	132.36	132.82
4.40	126.39	126.85	127.30	127.74	128.17	128.59	129.00	129.41
4.60	123.50	123.90	124.29	124.67	125.05	125.41	125.77	126.12
4.80	120.69	121.03	121.37	121.70	122.02	122.34	122.64	122.94
5.00	117.97	118.26	118.55	118.83	119.10	119.37	119.62	119.88
5.20	115.33	115.57	115.81	116.05	116.27	116.49	116.71	116.92
5.40	112.77	112.97	113.16	113.35	113.54	113.72	113.89	114.06
5.60	110.29	110.44	110.60	110.75	110.89	111.03	111.17	111.30
5.80	107.88	108.00	108.11	108.22	108.33	108.44	108.54	108.64
6.00	105.54	105.62	105.70	105.78	105.85	105.93	106.00	106.06
6.10	104.40	104.46	104.53	104.59	104.64	104.70	104.76	104.81
6.20	103.27	103.32	103.37	103.41	103.45	103.50	103.54	103.58
6.30	102.17	102.20	102.23	102.26	102.28	102.31	102.34	102.36
6.40	101.08	101.09	101.11	101.12	101.13	101.15	101.16	101.17
6.50	100.00	100.00	100.00	100.00	100.00	100.00	100.00	100.00
6.60	98.94	98.93	98.91	98.90	98.89	98.87	98.86	98.85
6.70	97.90	97.87	97.84	97.81	97.79	97.76	97.74	97.72
6.80	96.87	96.83	96.79	96.75	96.71	96.67	96.64	96.60
6.90	95.86	95.80	95.75	95.70	95.65	95.60	95.55	95.51
7.00	94.86	94.79	94.72	94.66	94.60	94.54	94.48	94.43
7.10	93.87	93.79	93.72	93.64	93.57	93.50	93.43	93.37
7.20	92.90	92.81	92.73	92.64	92.56	92.48	92.40	92.33
7.30	91.95	91.85	91.75	91.65	91.56	91.47	91.39	91.30
7.40	91.01	90.90	90.79	90.68	90.58	90.48	90.39	90.30
7.50	90.08	89.96	89.84	89.72	89.61	89.51	89.40	89.31
7.60	89.17	89.03	88.91	88.78	88.66	88.55	88.44	88.33
7.70	88.27	88.12	87.99	87.85	87.73	87.60	87.49	87.37
7.80	87.38	87.23	87.08	86.94	86.81	86.68	86.55	86.43
7.90	86.51	86.34	86.19	86.04	85.90	85.76	85.63	85.50
8.00	85.64	85.47	85.31	85.16	85.01	84.86	84.72	84.59
8.10	84.79	84.62	84.45	84.28	84.13	83.97	83.83	83.69
8.20	83.96	83.77	83.59	83.42	83.26	83.10	82.95	82.81
8.30	83.13	82.94	82.75	82.58	82.41	82.24	82.09	81.94
8.40	82.32	82.12	81.93	81.74	81.57	81.40	81.24	81.08
8.50	81.51	81.31	81.11	80.92	80.74	80.57	80.40	80.24
8.60	80.72	80.51	80.31	80.11	79.93	79.75	79.58	79.41
8.70	79.94	79.73	79.52	79.32	79.13	78.94	78.77	78.60
8.80	79.18	78.95	78.74	78.53	78.34	78.15	77.97	77.79
8.90	78.42	78.19	77.97	77.76	77.56	77.37	77.18	77.00
9.00	77.67	77.44	77.21	77.00	76.79	76.60	76.41	76.23
9.10	76.94	76.70	76.47	76.25	76.04	75.84	75.65	75.46
9.20	76.21	75.97	75.73	75.51	75.29	75.09	74.90	74.71
9.30	75.49	75.25	75.01	74.78	74.56	74.36	74.16	73.97
9.40	74.79	74.54	74.29	74.06	73.84	73.63	73.43	73.24
9.50	74.09	73.84	73.59	73.36	73.13	72.92	72.71	72.52
9.60	73.41	73.15	72.90	72.66	72.43	72.22	72.01	71.81
9.70	72.73	72.47	72.21	71.97	71.74	71.52	71.31	71.12
9.80	72.06	71.79	71.54	71.30	71.06	70.84	70.63	70.43
9.90	71.40	71.13	70.87	70.63	70.39	70.17	69.96	69.75
10.00	70.76	70.48	70.22	69.97	69.73	69.51	69.29	69.09
10.20	69.48	69.20	68.94	68.69	68.44	68.22	68.00	67.79
10.40	68.25	67.96	67.69	67.44	67.19	66.96	66.74	66.53
10.60	67.04	66.76	66.48	66.22	65.98	65.74	65.52	65.31
10.80	65.87	65.58	65.31	65.04	64.79	64.56	64.33	64.12
11.00	64.73	64.44	64.16	63.90	63.65	63.41	63.18	62.97
11.20	63.62	63.33	63.05	62.78	62.53	62.29	62.07	61.85
11.40	62.54	62.25	61.96	61.70	61.45	61.21	60.98	60.77
11.60	61.49	61.19	60.91	60.64	60.39	60.15	59.93	59.71
11.80	60.47	60.17	59.89	59.62	59.37	59.13	58.90	58.69
12.00	59.47	59.17	58.89	58.62	58.37	58.13	57.91	57.70

The "yield to maturity" can be found quickly in a bond values book.

are expressed in whole percentages and smaller measurements known as "basis points." A basis point is 1/100th of 1%. In other words, 100 basis points equals 1%. For example, a bond yield of 7.63% is 5 basis points less than a bond yield of 7.68%. The page to the left shows a sample table taken from a bond value book.

If the Exxon bond were under consideration, the buyer would first locate the 6½% coupon rate shown above in the upper left hand corner. Next, the buyer would locate the price closest to the expected purchase price in the column of prices appearing under the actual number of years to maturity; in this case, 1977 to 1998 or 21 years. The price $85.00 falls between the prices 85.76 and 84.86 which, in the far left column, correspond to yields of 7.90% and 8.00%. A more exact yield, can be found by interpolation. Therefore, because the bond price is now $85 (below par), the yield to maturity is greater than the 7.6% current yield.

Besides providing a more accurate picture of a buyer's potential return, yield to maturity also makes it possible to compare bonds of varying maturities and coupons. But even yield to maturity cannot be used blindly because a bond may be "called" before reaching the maturity date which can change the yield significantly.

Calling "Calling" a bond means the issuer exercises a right stated on the face of the bond to retire the bond before its maturity date. Most bonds are now issued with call provisions. The right to call a bond gives the issuer greater flexibility to respond to changes in the general level of interest rates. For example, if a corporation had issued bonds with a 10% coupon during a period of high interest rates, and if interest rates subsequently declined to a level where the same bond could be issued with an 8% coupon, it would be to the corporation's advantage to retire the 10% bonds and reissue new bonds at 8%. In fact, the annual interest savings can be so significant, often measured in millions of dollars, that issuers usually redeem the bonds at a premium above face value. Typically, the premium amounts to one year's annual interest. Thus, a $1,000, 10% bond might be called at $1,100.

Most bonds are not subject to call until a specified number of years have elapsed, say 5 or 10. After that period, the bonds can be called at any time at one specified price or the issuer can stipulate a declining scale of prices, one for each year remaining after the first call date.

In addition to the optional call method, many bonds and preferred stocks are also retired through the use of a "sinking fund."

Once established, the issuer must set aside a certain number of dollars each year for periodic retirements. This enhances the security of the remaining bonds. When new bonds are being issued, investment bankers often say they are "floating" a new issue; so it is understandable that a bond retirement fund be called a "sinking" fund. The bonds or preferred stock to be retired each year can either be called at a specific price or they can be purchased in the open market. Occasionally, the sinking fund payments are allowed to accumulate while earning interest, so the entire issue can eventually be retired at one time.

If bonds are called unexpectedly, a bondholder might get the principal amount back sooner, but lose what may have been an attractive yield. In some cases, the bondholder may even lose part of the principal. This would occur if a bond had been purchased at a substantial premium but called at a price close to par. For these reasons, the potential bond buyer should carefully examine call and sinking fund provisions with a broker or bond dealer to better understand the risks involved.

So far, it has been shown that bond selection must include a consideration of the type of issuer, maturity, coupon, yield, and call features. There is yet another important factor which must be included — a bond's "rating."

Ratings Ratings measure the probability of a bond issuer repaying the principal amount at maturity and meeting the scheduled interest payments. Viewed another way, ratings rank issues according to their perceived risk of default. They are computed and published by objective, independent organizations. The two best known rating agencies are Standard & Poor's Corporation and Moody's Investor Service Incorporated. Their ratings are available on a subscription basis and in a variety of publications that can usually be found at a local library or brokerage office.

Together, the two agencies rate most of the publicly held corporate and municipal bonds. In addition, Moody's rates many Treasury and government agency issues. They do not, however, rate privately placed bonds, unless they are asked to on a fee basis. In recent years, nearly 50 per cent of all bond issues have been placed privately which simply means that investors, usually institutions, have purchased the bonds directly from the issuer without any public distribution. Although preferred stocks have ratings which appear identical to bond ratings, they are not directly comparable because bonds represent debt and preferred stocks are equity (ownership).

The rating agencies use a simple system of letters to indicate their judgment of an issue's safety of principal and interest payment stability. Standard & Poor's ranks bonds from highest quality to lowest by using the first four letters of the alphabet in groups of three, as follows: AAA, AA, A, BBB, BB, B and so on through D. Bonds carrying a D rating are in default. Investors commonly refer to the highest rating as "Triple-A." Moody's uses a similar system, stopping at C, as follows: Aaa, Aa, A, Baa, Ba, B, Caa, Ca, C. Some of the bonds in Moody's C categories may be in default.

When appropriate, both agencies use other symbols to further refine a given rating. Thus, Standard & Poor's may add a plus or a minus sign to a rating. For example, an A+ rating is a shade higher than an A rating. In its municipal bond ratings, Moody's uses A1 and Baa1 to indicate the highest quality bonds falling within those two specific categories.

In both systems, rating groups from Triple-A through B carry the same meaning. Thus, Moody's opinion of an Aa bond is basically identical to Standard & Poor's opinion of its AA bond. Further, both systems clearly have a boundary line established with the BBB and Baa ratings which are the first categories indicating some speculative investment characteristics. Bonds above

BBB are believed safe investment candidates for both individuals and institutions. Bonds below BBB should receive careful analysis because they are inherently more speculative.

But ratings are more than interesting academic notations. They are gauges of risk and, in the marketplace, investors demand greater returns as risk increases. Thus, the lower an issuer's rating, the greater the annual interest payments demanded.

Since ratings can translate into millions of dollars of interest savings, the rating agencies are understandably thorough in researching their opinions. Each agency employs a staff of security analysts who examine the financial condition, operations and management of a given issuer. They also study specific documents such as the bond's "indenture" which describes certain legal and technical details of the issue. Perhaps the most important factor is an evaluation of the company's future earning's potential which calls for analytical techniques like those used in appraising common stocks. In general, bond analysts test an issuer's strength under adverse business conditions with an objective to determine the safety of principal and interest payments. After a rating is given, it is reviewed periodically and sometimes changed to reflect any improvement or deterioration in an issuer's overall condition.

In the New York Exchange bond room
before the move to new quarters in 1977.

135

Convertible Bonds Convertible bonds, as these debentures are commonly called, are usually subordinate to other debt. However, they have all the features discussed thus far — a par value, coupon rate, maturity date, yield and often a rating and a call date. But they differ from other bonds in one important respect. They can be converted into a specific number of shares of the issuer's common stock. Convertibility closely links the price performance of the bond with that of the underlying common stock. Thus, although a convertible bond offers some of the relative safety of principal and interest characteristic of so-called "straight" or non-convertible bonds, they usually fluctuate in price more widely and more rapidly due to the convertible feature. In this sense, convertible bondholders participate directly in the changing business fortunes of an issuer whereas other bondholders cannot. In short, convertible buyers give up some safety and interest in exchange for potential capital gains.

Corporations select convertibles to raise additional capital for several reasons. Convertibles, as opposed to a new common stock issue, limit the dilution of existing stockholders' equity. Convertibles also offer tax savings to the issuer because interest payments on convertibles,

and on other bonds, are deductions before Federal income taxes, while cash dividends are paid from after-tax earnings. Finally, the interest rates on convertibles usually yield more than equivalent common stock dividends but less than comparable straight bonds. If interest rates in the conventional bond market are high, an issuer can frequently obtain a lower rate by offering the convertibility feature as a sweetener.

Convertibles may offer an attractive opportunity for capital gains as well as income but they also place greater demands on the investor's analytical resources. Several new terms and calculations, which will be presented in the hypothetical example to follow, must be understood before convertibles can be used effectively.

Consider a 7% convertible subordinated debenture with 10 years remaining to maturity convertible into common stock at $40. The bond is currently selling at 90 ($900). The underlying common stock is selling for $32 a share.

The investor first must determine the maximum exposure to loss by calculating the bond's price as if it were selling as a "straight" bond. This price, often called the "investment value," is usually computed by the same organizations that publish bond

A convertible bond is one of the
most complicated securities
to use effectively.

ratings. The investment value is that price which causes the bond's yield to maturity to equal the yields offered by straight bonds of similar quality and maturity. Suppose our bond carries a Baa rating (convertibles rarely receive higher) and that straight bonds in this category are currently yielding 9%. The appropriate calculations indicate that our bond must sell for approximately $835 to yield 9%.

The investment value represents the theoretical downside risk, the floor beyond which the bond's price should not fall in the current market environment. Again, it is theoretical and based on comparative values which are subject to change. In this case, however, it does tell the investor that, without its convertible feature, the bond could decline roughly 7% from the purchase price to its value as a straight bond.

Next, the convertible buyer will want to compare this risk with the possible reward.

Since the $1,000 bond is convertible into common stock at $40, the investor knows that each bond has a "conversion ratio" of 25. In other words, at the $40 "conversion price" each bond can be exchanged for 25 shares of common stock ($1,000 divided by $40 = 25). Although the bond is convertible at $40, the stock is actually being bought at $36 because the same conversion privilege

is being obtained at a discount. This price is called the stock's "conversion parity price." It is obtained by dividing the bond's actual purchase price by the number of shares that will be received upon conversion ($900 divided by 25 = $36). Viewed another way, at the conversion parity price, the investor breaks even. As the stock's price advances beyond conversion parity, the bond's value should follow step with at least an equal percentage move. In this case, the conversion parity price of $36 is roughly 12% higher than the stock's current price of $32.

From the breakeven point, the buyer now explores the potential gain which might ultimately be realized. The investor should have some reasonable profit target in mind. Assume the bond investor concludes, after a thorough study of the issuer's business and prospects, that the common stock will rise to $50. At $50 per share, the bond would be worth $1,250 (25 shares x $50 per share = $1,250) representing a profit of nearly 40% on the $900 investment. In addition, the investor receives a steady stream of interest payments.

The sophisticated convertible buyer attempts to limit risk by selecting a bond where:

- The current price is close to the investment value,

- The conversion parity price is close to the common stock's current price,

- The common stock is expected to appreciate considerably.

Rarely, however, are actual situations as clearly defined as this example. A convertible bond is one of the most complicated securities to use effectively.

Municipal Bonds

Municipal bonds are issued by states, cities, towns, political subdivisions or authorities, such as housing authorities and bridge and tunnel authorities. They are usually issued to finance new construction for such diverse purposes as hospitals, bridges, tunnels and sports stadiums.

Municipal bonds differ from straight corporate bonds in three ways. First, and most important, the interest on municipals is exempt from Federal income taxes. Further, if the investor lives in the state of issue, they are usually exempt from state and local taxes as well. This tax exempt feature sets municipal bonds apart from all other bonds and explains why municipals are frequently called "tax exempts."

Secondly, municipals are usually issued with "serial" maturities as opposed to the "term" maturities characteristic of corporate bonds. Serial maturity means that a portion of the total issue matures annually until the entire issue is retired. Unlike sinking fund retirements, each year in a serial issue has its own interest rate or is priced to provide a specific yield. In October, 1976, for example, the State of Maryland issued $145 million of 15-year Triple-A general obligation bonds at a net interest cost of 4.86%. The bonds were reoffered to

If your Taxable Income* is:		Then Your Tax Bracket is:	A Tax Exempt Yield of:				
Joint Return	Single Return		4%	5%	6%	7%	8%
			is equal to a taxable yield of:				
$ 16- 20,000		28%	5.56%	6.94%	8.33%	9.72%	11.11%
	$14-16,000	31%	5.80	7.25	8.70	10.14	11.59
$ 24- 28,000	$18-20,000	36%	6.25	7.81	9.38	10.94	12.50
$ 36- 40,000	$26-32,000	45%	7.27	9.09	10.91	12.73	14.55
$ 44- 52,000	$32-38,000	50%	8.00	10.00	12.00	14.00	16.00
$ 64- 76,000	$38-44,000	55%	8.89	11.11	13.33	15.56	17.78
$ 88-100,000	$44-50,000	60%	10.00	12.50	15.00	17.50	20.00
$100-120,000	$50-60,000	62%	10.53	13.16	15.79	18.42	21.05

Net amount subject to Federal Income Tax after deductions and exemptions.

investors on the following partial "scale," as the series of yields is known: 1977 priced to yield 3.70%, 1980 to yield 3.90%, 1981 to yield 4.10% and ending with a 5.20% yield in 1991.

Thirdly, most municipals are issued in $5,000 principal amounts, whereas corporate bonds usually have a $1,000 principal amount. Further, municipal bonds are traded entirely in the over-the-counter market unlike corporate bonds which are also listed on some of the national exchanges. An investor interested in a specific issue must consult a bond dealer for a price. Municipal prices are usually not quoted in daily newspapers. The dealers themselves frequently consult The Blue List of Current Municipal Offerings, a daily publication, which gives pertinent data such as price and yield on available offerings. Although municipals usually have a $5,000 principal amount, their prices are nonetheless quoted as if the principal amount was $1,000 (i.e. at 100 or some premium or discount to 100).

There are several types of municipal bonds. Most common is the General Obligation Bond where the issuer promises full faith, credit and taxing power to insure that principal and interest payments are made on time. These general obligation bonds

are considered to provide the greatest security and, as a result, usually have the lowest yields. Revenue bonds, are backed only by the earning power of the facility constructed with the proceeds of the bond issue. Other types include general obligation bonds with a provision limiting the amount of taxation which can be applied, special tax bonds, and industrial revenue bonds.

In general, because of the tax exempt feature, municipal bonds have interest rates several percentage points below the going rate on corporate bonds of comparable quality. In other words, a municipal bond will often provide the same after-tax yield to an investor as a corporate bond priced to yield several points more. The benefit of this tax exempt feature improves as an investor's annual taxable income and tax bracket increases. For example, the tax bracket for a husband and wife filing a joint return with a $20,000 taxable income has been roughly 28%. To equal a 5% municipal bond yield, they would have to find a corporate bond yielding approximately 7%. By comparison, an investor in a 60% tax bracket earning $100,000 must find a corporate bond yielding roughly 13% to get the same after-tax return that a municipal bond can offer.

...the interest on municipals
is exempt from Federal
income taxes.

Preferred Stocks At first glance, many preferred stocks might appear to be bonds without a maturity date. They offer relatively attractive yields, they can be called, some can be converted into common stock, some are rated, most are issued at a stated par value (usually $100) and all are commonly listed as "senior securities." Indeed, some preferred stocks are thought to be of such high quality, that their prices tend to parallel the price trends of high quality, long term bonds.

There are, however, several important distinctions which investors should appreciate before buying preferreds:

(1) Dividends — Although the dividend is set at a fixed annual rate, it can be changed by the issuer at any time. It can, in fact, be omitted entirely. For this reason, most investors seek a "cumulative preferred stock" which means that if dividends are "passed" by the board of directors, they are allowed to accumulate and must eventually be paid when money becomes available.

(2) Claims — As the name implies, a preferred stock has preference over the common stock in the receipt of dividends and in any residual assets after payments to creditors should the company be dissolved. But a creditor, such as a bondholder, has a legally enforceable claim against an issuer who defaults on an interest payment. A preferred stockholder has no such claim should a dividend be omitted.

"Participating" preferred stocks enable the owner to share in any extra dividend payments, although most preferreds are "nonparticipating," which limits the annual return to the fixed annual dividend payment.

Corporations have favored bonds over preferred stocks as a method of raising new capital. Preferred dividends are paid from after-tax earnings whereas bond interest is paid from earnings before taxes. Thus, preferred stocks can be more expensive to the corporation.

A preferred stock is a blend of the characteristics of a bond and a common stock. It can offer the higher yield of a bond; it has priority over the common in equity ownership, but it does not have the safety of a bond and its participation in the company's growth is limited.

Preferred stocks are usually bought for income. The investor should strive for high income with greater safety (a preferred with little debt ahead of it) or high income with growth (a preferred convertible into common stock). Otherwise, it is probably better to own the bond or the common stock.

U.S. Government Securities —
A Treasury Bond, a Treasury
Note and a Treasury Bill.

141

United States Government Securities The
Federal government, much like state and
local governments, also uses debt obligations to finance various projects and programs. Three types, generally differentiated according to maturity range, are used
most frequently. They are: *Treasury bills,*
with maturities up to and including one
year; *Treasury notes,* with maturities
between one year and seven years; and
U.S. government bonds, with maturities
between seven years and twenty-five years.
There can be exceptions to this general
classification, however. For example, the
Treasury recently issued 10-year, 8% notes.

Government securities offer the investor:

- Maximum safety of principal since they
  are backed by the word of the government itself;

- Competitive yields, although seldom
  equal to yields on less-secure corporate bonds;

- A high degree of liquidity through
  active trading in secondary markets
  both listed and over-the-counter;

- Limited taxation because they are free
  of state and local taxes, although not
  from federally imposed taxes.

Treasury bills, commonly called "T-bills,"
account for the bulk of government financing. They are sold by the Treasury at a discount through competitive bidding. A
weekly auction is held for bills with three-
month and six-month maturities. Monthly
auctions are held for the remaining two maturities — nine-month and one-year bills.
Treasury bills are issued in five denominations from $10,000 to $1,000,000. The return
to the investor is the difference between the
purchase price and the bill's face value received at maturity. Bills can be sold in the
secondary market before maturity. Individuals can purchase bills directly at no
charge either from a Federal Reserve Bank
or the Bureau of the Public Debt by sending a certified personal check or cashier's
check for the bill's face value to:

Bureau of the Public Debt,
Securities Transactions Branch,
Washington, D.C. 20226.

Details are provided in the Addendum on
pages 213 to 215.

Bills can also be purchased for a fee
from certain commercial banks, government securities dealers and brokerage
firms. As discussed later, T-bills are
the major vehicle used by the Federal
Reserve System in the money market to
implement national monetary policy.

Treasury notes have become increasingly popular with individual investors for three reasons. First, they are usually issued in $1,000 denominations which is more affordable than the $10,000 minimum T-bill investment. Secondly, their longer maturities usually offer higher yields than T-bills. And, finally, notes are now being issued more frequently.

Notes have a fixed rate of interest payable semiannually, and can be purchased without charge at issuance from Federal Reserve Banks or their branches or from the Treasury itself by writing to the Bureau of the Public Debt. Investors can also buy them for a fee from some commercial banks, brokerage houses and other government securities dealers.

Government bonds can also be purchased without charge at issuance directly from the Treasury and Federal Reserve Banks often in denominations as low as $1,000. In many ways, they resemble straight corporate bonds. They have fixed rates of interest and fixed maturity dates and some are callable. If a bond is callable, its maturity date will appear in newspaper bond tables in hyphenated form. For example, 1988-93, means that the bond matures in 1993 but can be called as early as 1988.

Many investors were first exposed to government bonds through the famous Series E Savings Bond used during World War II. Series E and the related Series H bonds are still offered today but in recent years they have seldom constituted a meaningful part of investment portfolios due to the relatively low annual return they provide.

Nearly twenty other government agencies issue short-term notes, debentures and participation certificates to finance their specialized operations. Most "agencies" have maturity dates, fixed interest rates and face values, but are rarely callable. Unlike the direct obligations of the U. S. Treasury, however, only a few agencies are backed by the Federal government. As a result, they usually offer higher yields than Treasury issues. The best known agency issues are sold by the Federal National Mortgage Association and the Government National Mortgage Association, commonly called "Fannie Mae" and "Ginnie Mae." In general, these two agencies strengthen the market for certain types of mortgages.

The Money Market Securities comprising the capital market primarily serve investors and borrowers who have a time horizon extending beyond one year. But many investors have surplus cash they want to employ for shorter time periods, even as short as overnight. Similarly, many borrowers need to raise money quickly for only short-term use. In both cases, the money market provides the ideal solution.

The money market is actually composed of several individual markets, one for each of its short-term credit instruments. Thus, there are markets for Treasury bills, commercial paper, negotiable certificates of deposit (CD's) and bankers' acceptances. In addition, commercial bank borrowings from each other at the "Federal Funds rate" and commercial bank borrowings from the Federal Reserve Banks at the "discount rate" are also considered important parts of the money market. Unlike the other transactions, however, neither method of bank borrowing creates "negotiable paper" (marketable promissory notes pledging the return of principal at maturity and fixed interest payments in the meantime).

In any case, all transactions have maturities within one year and most are 90 days or less. Although each credit instrument is different, the rates tend to move closely together.

Investors, including commercial banks, state and local governments, some individuals, large non-financial businesses, foreign banks, and non-bank financial institutions, are drawn to the money market for three basic reasons in addition to attractive yields:

(1) It is a liquid market capable of handling billions of dollars with slight effects on yields.

(2) It offers a high degree of safety of principal because issuers, in general, have the highest credit ratings. Investors should realize, however, that certain credit instruments can never be considered completely risk free. When the Penn Central went bankrupt in 1970, for example, it had $82 million in commercial paper outstanding.

(3) Money market maturities are short and thus there is little risk of loss due to interest rate changes.

Borrowers, in turn, including the U.S. Treasury, commercial banks, and non-financial corporations, seek the market's attractive rates which are generally below bank loan rates even to prime borrowers.

By far the most important participant in the money market is the Federal Reserve System. Through its Open Market Trading

Desk at the New York Federal Reserve Bank, one of twelve Federal Reserve banks, the system implements the decisions of the Federal Open Market Committee. By selling and buying various money market instruments, the Federal Reserve contracts or expands the reserve positions of some 6,000 commercial banks that are members of the system. In this way, the Federal Reserve influences monetary and credit conditions of the entire country.

Rates on other money market instruments are generally scaled upward from the Treasury bill rate on comparable maturities. Otherwise, they could not compete with the nearly riskless and highly flexible government security.

Yields on negotiable certificates of deposit (CD's), for example, are usually several basis points higher. CD's are issued by banks. They are receipts for funds deposited with them for a predetermined period of time on which the bank agrees to pay a specific rate of interest. A CD returns principal and interest to the owner at maturity, but it can also be sold in a secondary market should the owner need the money before maturity. CD's are particularly popular with large corporations that use them in cash management as a back-up to Treasury bills.

Maturity dates are usually selected to suit the needs of the purchaser. They range between one and eighteen months, but most CD's mature in four months. CD's are issued in denominations from $25,000 to $10 million. In the secondary market, dealers usually trade in $1 million denominations.

Commercial paper is another money market instrument, although there is no secondary market. This instrument, sold in denominations from $5,000 to $5 million or more, is simply a short term promissory note credit worthy businesses use in place of bank borrowing because, traditionally, it has been less expensive.

Tax anticipation bills, bankers' acceptances and loans to and repurchase agreements with government securities dealers are also considered money market instruments. However, Treasury bills, CD's and commercial paper comprise the bulk of money market transactions.

Money market instruments, along with bonds and preferred stocks, play an important role in the world of investments. They can be, for many investors, either an effective complement or a valuable alternative to common stocks.

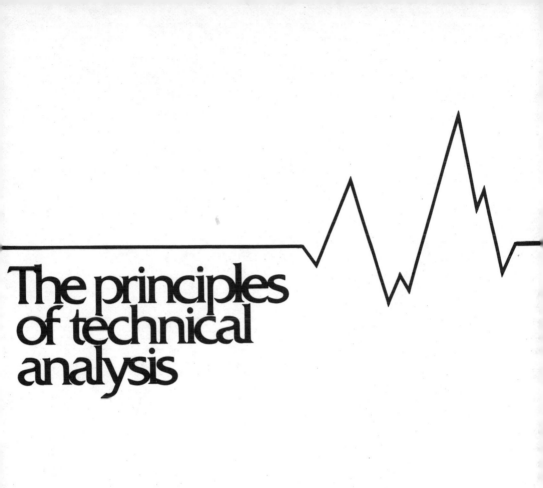

The principles
of technical
analysis

Introduction On Wall Street there are two distinct approaches to the stock market. "Fundamental Analysis" is the study of all relevant factors that can influence the future course of corporate earnings and dividends and, hence, stock prices. This approach involves the analysis of economic data, industry conditions, company fundamentals and corporate financial statements. In contrast, "Technical Analysis" is the study of all factors related to the actual supply and demand of stocks. Through the use of stock charts and various indicators, the technicians, as they are called, attempt to measure the "pulse of the market" and sometimes try to forecast future stock price movements.

The substantial number of investors successfully using fundamental analysis attests to the merits of their approach. However, technical analysis also has considerable value because, ironically, not all investors believe in it. A wise Wall Street observer once said "if everybody could buy at the bottom and sell at the top, the bottom would be the top and the top would be the bottom."

The individual who understands both fundamental and technical analysis knows the strengths and weaknesses of each approach and should, therefore, have an advantage on Wall Street.

This chapter will describe several popular technical methods and explain a few principles of technical analysis that have been successful over the years.

Bar Charts A stock chart is a picture of price history. With just a glance, an investor can quickly see the stock's past action and gain valuable perspective.

There are several types of stock charts. The most popular, called a "bar chart," shows the price of a stock and its volume (number of shares traded) over a period of time — usually measured in days, weeks or months. A daily bar chart, for example, would show the highest, lowest and closing prices each day as well as the number of shares traded daily. Similarly, a weekly bar chart would show the highest and lowest prices for the entire week as well as Friday's closing price and the total volume Monday through Friday.

To demonstrate how bar charts are constructed, assume that a stock traded at these prices over a period of four weeks (twenty trading days):

	Date	High	Low	Close	Volume
First	Mon. 2nd	29¾	28½	29	13,400
Week	Tues. 3rd	29½	28⅝	29⅛	15,200
	Weds. 4th	29½	28¼	28¾	15,800
	Thurs. 5th	29	27⅞	28½	17,500
	Fri. 6th	28⅝	27	27½	14,300
Second	Mon. 9th	29	26¾	29	40,200
Week	Tues. 10th	29½	28¾	29	16,100
	Weds. 11th	30¼	29	30	29,400
	Thurs. 12th	31	29⅝	30½	15,600
	Fri. 13th	30¾	30	30¼	12,100
Third	Mon. 16th	31	30⅛	30¾	17,800
Week	Tues. 17th	31½	30⅜	30⅜	10,200
	Weds. 18th	30¾	29½	29¾	18,100
	Thurs. 19th	30	29⅛	29¾	15,000
	Fri. 20th	29¾	29⅛	29⅝	13,100
Fourth	Mon. 23rd	32	29⅝	31¼	18,000
Week	Tues. 24th	32¼	31	31⅜	14,500
	Weds. 25th	32	31⅛	31⅞	14,900
	Thurs. 26th	32½	30¾	30¾	17,300
	Fri. 27th	31⅝	30⅜	31½	11,700

A daily bar chart of these prices would appear as follows:

A weekly bar chart of the same prices would be simply a condensed version of the daily chart:

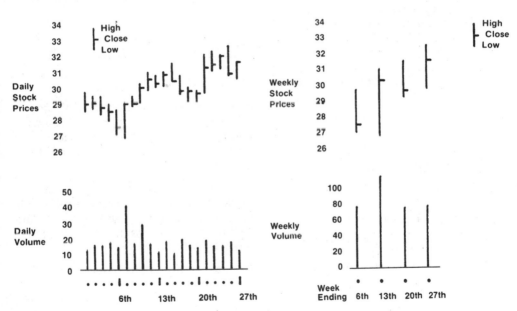

Chart Patterns Once a bar chart has been constructed and maintained over time various patterns appear. Each tells a different story and some are more valuable than others. "Support and resistance" patterns, for example, work well because investors have a tendency to remember past stock prices. Here are two typical support and resistance patterns and the psychological reasoning behind each:

Price Support

For several weeks or months this stock traded in a price range between $15 and $20 providing ample time for many investors to buy, sell or just observe. When the stock suddenly rose above $20, an action that is called a "breakout," each person who bought the stock was saying "Boy, am I smart! This is a good one! If it returns to the $15 to $20 range, I'll buy more." The same can be said for the investor who sold it or watched it rise without owning it. "What a mistake! If the stock returns to that price range again I'll buy it!"

The story would be completely different, of course, if the breakout happened to be down forming a price resistance pattern.

Price Resistance

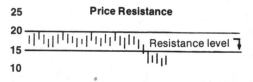

In this case, the stockholders might be thinking "I *knew* that stock should have been sold! If it rallies back to $15 to $20, I'm going to sell it and use the money to buy a better stock!"

Price support and price resistance patterns have greater meaning when the trading range is accompanied by large volume. This usually indicates that investment interest is high.

Normally, the moment the stock breaks out of its trading range — either up or down — volume increases. If it does, and the stock continues in the same direction, the pattern can be considered quite reliable.

There are two other types of support and resistance chart patterns:

Volume Support

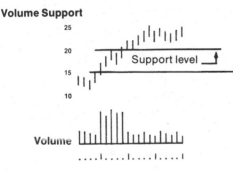

The increased volume, as illustrated above, highlights the accelerated trading activity at those particular price levels. For essentially the same psychological reasons mentioned earlier, support and resistance levels created by volume can also influence future buy and sell orders.

Volume Resistance

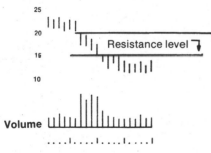

Ascending and descending triangles are interesting and useful variations of the price support and price resistance patterns discussed earlier. They are so named because the direction of the breakout is frequently indicated in advance by the shape of the triangle.

Ascending Triangle

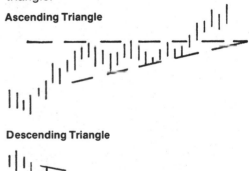

Descending Triangle

When the direction of a stock changes, specific chart patterns frequently develop as the turn occurs. Several of these so-called "reversal patterns" are shown on the next two pages. In some cases they develop gradually; at other times, the reversal occurs more suddenly.

Panic Reversal

Head & Shoulders Reversal

S   H   S

Neckline

Rounding Top Reversal

Descending Triangle Reversal

Double Top Reversal

1   2

Broadening Top Reversal

1   3   5

2   4

Selling Climax Reversal

Test

Climax

Inverse Head & Shoulders Reversal

— Neckline

S   S

H

Rounding Bottom Reversal

Ascending Triangle Reversal

Double Bottom Reversal

1   2

Triple Bottom Reversal

1   2   3

Breakaway Gap (up)

Breakaway Gap (down)

Runaway Gap

Exhaustion Gap

Island Reversal Gap

A "gap" occurs when the trading range on a given day is above or below the trading range of the previous day. Often the result of an emotional response to an overnight news item, a gap can be the first indication of a new price trend. However, if the stock's unusual volatility is partly due to a small float (i.e., a relatively small number of shares available for trading), the gap can be less reliable as a chart pattern.

Bar charts are amazingly geometric. As a result, technicians frequently draw trendlines and channels to identify future support and resistance points. In so doing, an experienced chartist will not ignore the "secondary points" which are the high and low points immediately before and after each peak or trough. Here are three trendline illustrations:

Trendline Support

Trendline Resistance

Trendline Resistance

Trendline Support

CHANNEL

Stock charts are like snow flakes — they are similar but never exactly the same. With the benefit of 20/20 hindsight and hours of experimenting an investor can apply many of the same lessons learned time after time. Still, stock patterns present two major problems:

- If the pattern has developed completely, some of the move has already occurred.
- Chart patterns are never 100% reliable.

Most technical analysts who use bar charts prefer the regular scale graph paper which is probably best for most investors. However, technicians interested in stock price movements on a percentage basis can obtain a somewhat different perspective by constructing the same charts on semi-logarithmic scale paper.

There are several reliable subscriptions available that provide charts of hundreds of companies in various formats. The samples on the next three pages show the same stock in different formats.

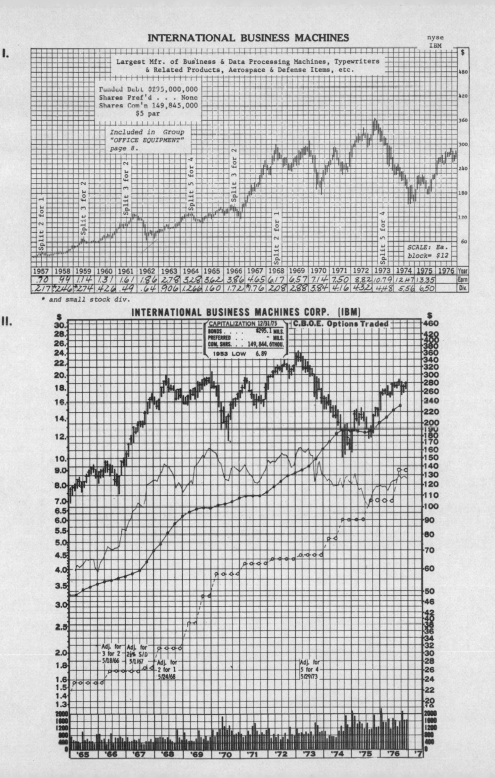

INTERNATIONAL BUSINESS MACHINES

nyse
IBM

I.

Largest Mfr. of Business & Data Processing Machines, Typewriters
& Related Products, Aerospace & Defense Items, etc.

Funded Debt 0295,000,000
Shares Pref'd . . . None
Shares Com'n 149,845,000
$5 par

Included in Group
"OFFICE EQUIPMENT"
page 8.

Split 2 for 1
Split 3 for 2
Split 3 for 2
Split 5 for 4
Split 3 for 2
Split 2 for 1
Split 5 for 4

SCALE: Ea.
block= $12

Year	1957	1958	1959	1960	1961	1962	1963	1964	1965	1966	1967	1968	1969	1970	1971	1972	1973	1974	1975	1976
Earn	.70	.99	1.14	1.31	1.61	1.86	2.78	3.28	3.62	3.86	4.65	6.17	6.57	7.14	7.50	8.82	10.79	12.47	13.35	
Div.	.217	.246	.274	.426	.49	.64	.906	1.266	1.60	1.72	*1.76	208	288	3.84	4.16	432	448	5.56	6.50	

* and small stock div.

II.

INTERNATIONAL BUSINESS MACHINES CORP. [IBM]

CAPITALIZATION 12/31/75
BONDS . . . . $295.1 MILS.
PREFERRED . . - MILS.
COM. SHRS. . . 149,844.6 THOU.
1953 LOW 6.89

C.B.O.E. Options Traded

Adj. for
3 for 2
5/18/66

Adj. for
2½% S/D
5/1/67

Adj. for
2 for 1
5/24/68

Adj. for
5 for 4
5/29/73

'65 '66 '67 '68 '69 '70 '71 '72 '73 '74 '75 '76 '7

III.

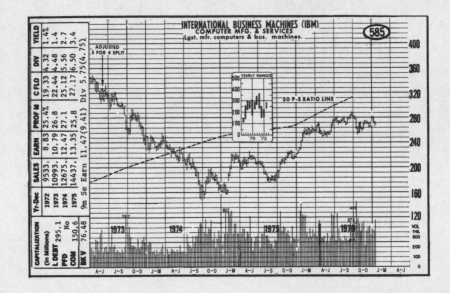

Int'l. Business Machine
OPTIONS-CBO

IBM

INTERNATIONAL BUSINESS MACHINES (IBM)
COMPUTER MFG. & SERVICES
Lgst. mfr. computers & bus. machines.

585

ADJUSTED
5 FOR 4 SPLIT

20 P-E RATIO LINE

YEARLY RANGES

IV.

CAPITALIZATION (In Millions)	Yr-Dec	SALES	EARN	PROF M	C FLO	DIV	YIELD
L DEBT 295.1	1972	9533.	8.83	25.4%	19.33	4.32	1.4%
PFD No	1973	10993.	10.79	26.8	22.44	4.48	1.4
COM 150.6	1974	12675.	12.47	27.1	25.12	5.56	2.7
BK V 76.48	1975	14437.	13.35	25.8	27.17	6.50	3.4

9m Se Earn 11.47(9.41)   Div 5.75(4.75)

V.

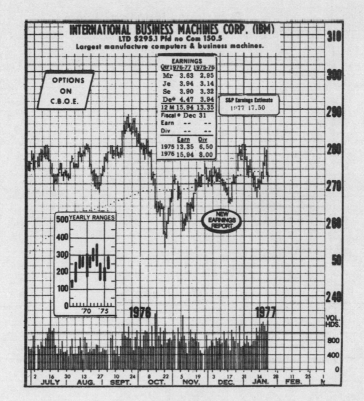

I. **The Stock Picture**
   M. C. Horsey & Company, Inc.
   120 South Blvd.
   Salisbury, Md. 21801

II. **3-Trend Cycli-Graphs**
   Securities Research Company
   208 Newbury Street
   Boston, Mass. 02116

III. **Mansfield Stock Chart Service**
   R. W. Mansfield Company
   26 Journal Square
   Jersey City, New Jersey 07306

IV. **Trendline's Current Market Perspectives**

   Standard & Poor's Corporation
   25 Broadway
   New York, N.Y. 10004

V. **Daily Basis Stock Charts**

   Standard & Poor's Corporation
   25 Broadway
   New York, N.Y. 10004

Dow Jones Industrial Average

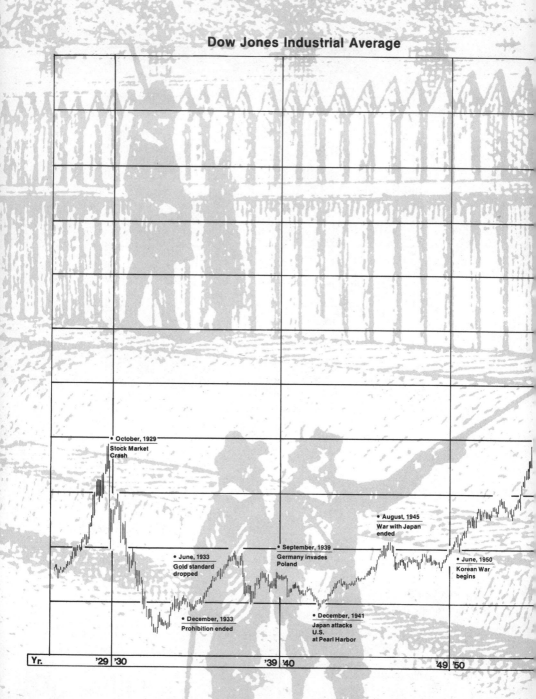

- October, 1929
Stock Market Crash

- August, 1945
War with Japan ended

- June, 1933
Gold standard dropped

- September, 1939
Germany invades Poland

- June, 1950
Korean War begins

- December, 1933
Prohibition ended

- December, 1941
Japan attacks U.S. at Pearl Harbor

Yr. '29 '30   '39 '40   '49 '50

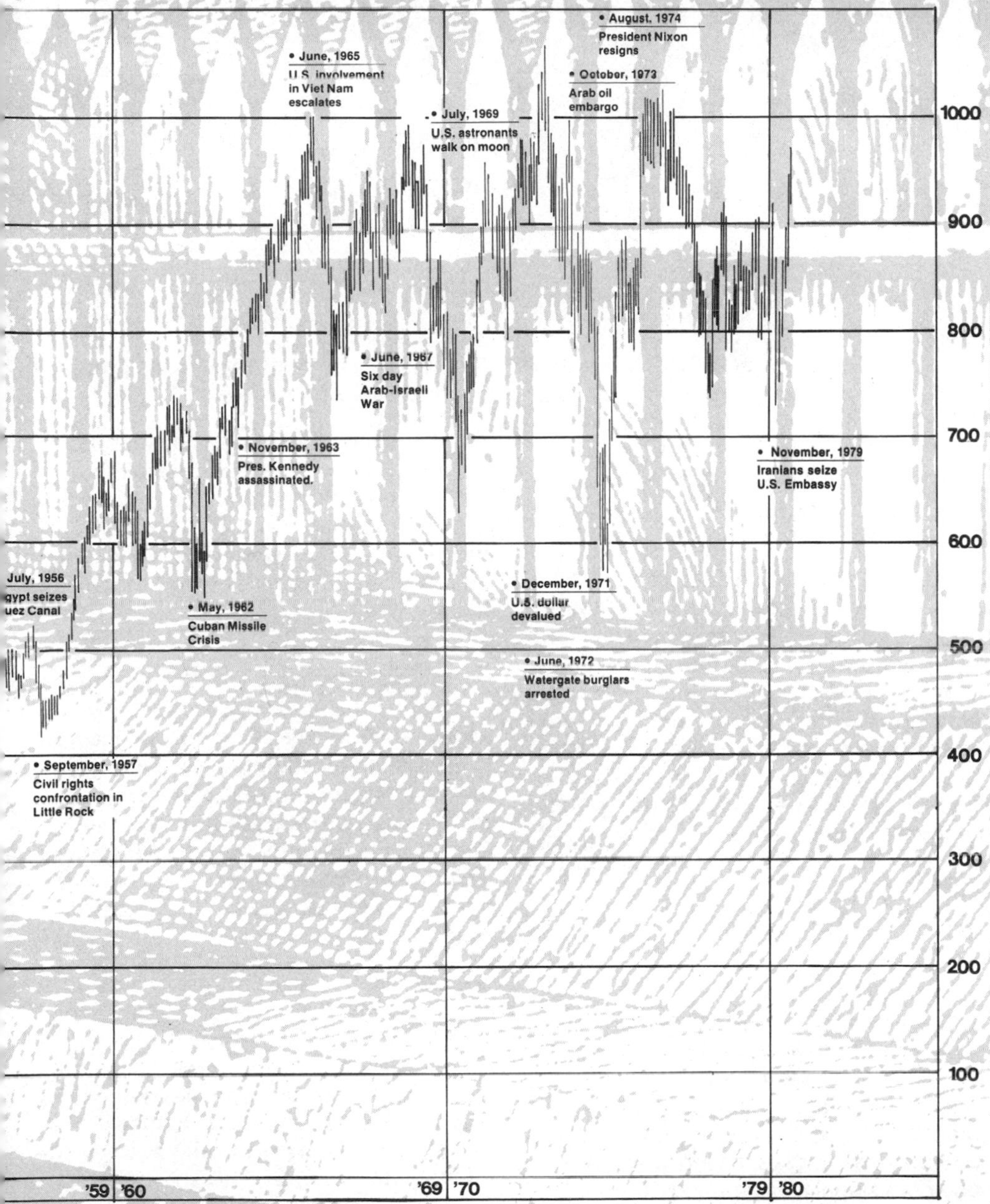
• August, 1974
President Nixon resigns
• June, 1965
U.S. involvement in Viet Nam escalates
• October, 1973
Arab oil embargo
• July, 1969
U.S. astronants walk on moon
1000
900
800
• June, 1967
Six day Arab-Israeli War
700
• November, 1963
Pres. Kennedy assassinated.
• November, 1979
Iranians seize U.S. Embassy
600
July, 1956
gypt seizes
uez Canal
• May, 1962
Cuban Missile Crisis
• December, 1971
U.S. dollar devalued
500
• June, 1972
Watergate burglars arrested
400
• September, 1957
Civil rights confrontation in Little Rock
300
200
100
'59
'60
'69
'70
'79
'80

The Dow Theory The Dow Theory is one of the oldest and most famous technical tools of the stock market. Its primary purpose is to forecast the future direction of the overall stock market by using, as a guide, the past actions of both the Dow Jones Industrial Average and the Dow Jones Transportation Average.

The Dow Theory is based mainly on the observation that market movements are analogous to movements of the sea. In other words, there are three movements in the market, all occurring simultaneously: Hourly or daily fluctuations (ripples); Secondary or intermediate movements of two or three weeks to a month or more (waves) and the primary trend extending several months to a year or more (the tide). It is this primary trend that is generally referred to as either a bull or bear market.

According to early proponents of the Theory, daily fluctuations are of little value. Secondary movements, however, are closely watched. They can retrace between one-third and two-thirds of the prior primary price change. The Dow Theory becomes useful when the secondary movements of the Dow Jones Industrial Average and the Dow Jones Transportation Average both signal a new primary trend by penetrating their previous secondary peak points. A new primary trend is not "confirmed" until both averages have produced the necessary signal.

Although most technicians believe the Dow Theory has been successful, they do not agree to what extent. The distinction between a primary and a secondary movement is not always clear. Still, many analysts find the tenets of the Theory useful in their work.

The Moving Average Deviation Technicians frequently watch a stock's progress by relating the stock price to its "moving average." A 30-week average, for example, is calculated by adding the stock's closing price of the current week to the closing prices of the previous twenty-nine weeks and dividing by thirty. As time passes, the weekly average becomes a "moving average" which shows a smoothed trend of past prices.

A stock's momentum, or rate of change, is shown by its "Moving Average Deviation." Using a weekly chart and a 10-week moving average of the stock price, an investor can, each week, calculate the deviation by simply dividing the last stock price in the series by the 10-week moving average calculated for that week. This approach can be especially helpful in the technical analysis of highly volatile stocks (e.g., many growth and cyclical stocks). A new price trend is often indicated by the moving average deviation well before it actually takes place. It is also a good measure of an "over bought" and "over sold" condition that can result when a stock moves too far too quickly.

A weekly Moving Average Deviation chart would look like this:

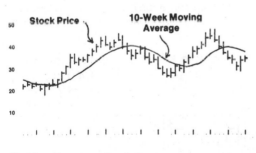

Moving Average Deviation

Sometimes calculating a 10-week moving average *of the deviation* and plotting it on the same (lower) scale will help the investor maintain a longer term perspective and avoid being "whipsawed" by excessive short term activity.

Beta Many professional portfolio managers use a form of technical analysis in their attempt to measure a stock's market risk or sensitivity by calculating its "beta coefficient." Beta is a measure of the average percentage change in the price of a stock relative to the percentage change of a market index.

Usually beta is computed relative to the S & P Index (i.e., the S & P Index = 1.00). A typical electronics stock, for example, might have a beta of 1.60 while a bank stock or an electric utility could have a beta of only .80 or less. Generally, the higher the beta, the more volatile the stock.

Portfolio managers often try to outperform the market by placing high-beta stocks into the portfolio when the market is expected to advance and by using low-beta stocks when they think the market outlook is less promising.

The major drawback to beta analysis is that beta never remains constant and predicting its future direction can be hazardous. As a result, beta is a highly controversial subject on Wall Street.

Point & Figure Charts Quite different from bar charting is another method called "point and figure" analysis. Although point and figure cannot measure time precisely and does not show volume which are two important features of bar charts, it has its advantages. Construction is simple and, once understood, a point and figure chart is easy to maintain and read. As with bar charts, an investor should spend at least several hours experimenting with old charts before any theories are put into practice.

Prior to starting a point and figure chart, examine the past price range and volatility of the stock. It is necessary to determine the appropriate denomination or "reversal" to be used on the chart. A high-priced stock (e.g., $50 or above) usually requires a 2 point, 3 point, or perhaps a 5 point reversal. A medium-priced stock (say, in the $20 to $50 range) is probably best represented by a 1 point, a 1½ point, or 2 point reversal chart. A ½ point or a 1 point reversal is frequently used to chart low-priced stocks. Any one of these reversals will work on the same stock but the chartist must decide which is most effective. With point and figure charts, the stock moves in only one direction at a time — up or down. It does not change direction until a "reversal" of the desired amount occurs.

Once the scale has been drawn, mark the beginning price on the chart. If the price advances thereafter, place X's on top of one another. If the price declines, use O's placing them below one another. These symbols are used merely to identify the price direction. When the stock's direction changes by the required amount (the reversal), move to the next column. Do not place a new "X" or "O" on the chart until the exact price has been hit. As time passes, the result will be alternating columns of X's and O's.

For example, shown below is a 2 point reversal chart built from this string of prices: 29 (start), 32¾, 29⅝, 33¼, 30⅛, 34⅞.

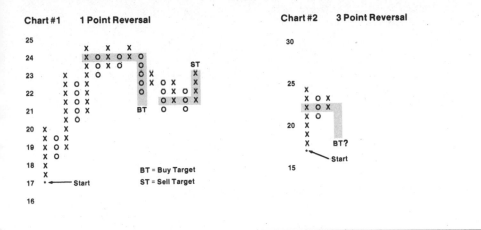

Chart #1   1 Point Reversal

BT = Buy Target
ST = Sell Target

Chart #2   3 Point Reversal

BT?
Start

Point and figure charts, similar to bar charts, can show price support levels and price resistance levels. In addition, "break-outs" are easy to detect using the point and figure method:

Bullish

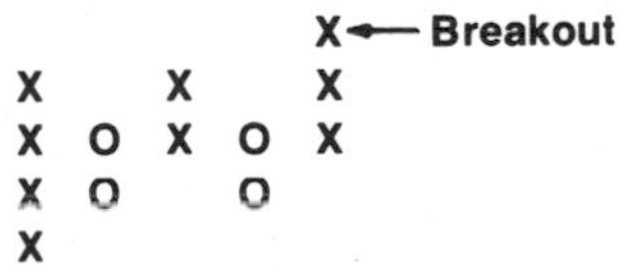

X ← Breakout

Bearish

O ← Breakout

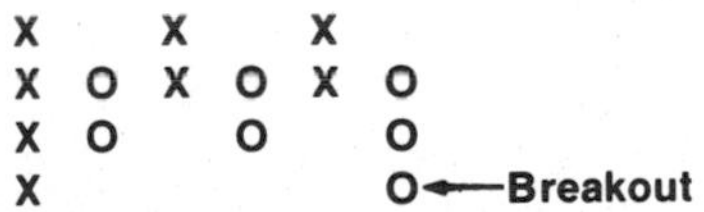

Many technicians use point and figure charts to predict how far a stock can advance or decline. There are several techniques although none has been found to work every time.

The charts labeled #1 and #2 at the top of the page illustrate one approach. Both charts above are constructed from this same string of prices: 17 (start), 20⅜, 18⅛, 20¾, 19⅝, 23¼, 21½, 20¼, 24⅝, 22¾, 24¾, 23⅛, 24¾, 22, 23⅛, 20¾, 22½, 20⅝, 23¼.

According to point and figure practitioners, the greater the frequency of reversals at a certain level, the greater the stock's potential rise or fall from that level. As the 1 point reversal chart demonstrates, the base indicating the 21 Buy Target has a count of *six* (shaded) across the 24 line. Six blocks below is the 21 price objective. Similarly, the Sell Target of 23½ is the result of a base count of *four* (shaded) across the 21½ line. The base to be used in the measurement can be found at the foot of the breakout regardless of whether the chartist is looking for a buy target or a sell target.

Point and figure charts can do many things. They can help an investor spot breakouts and new price trends. They can help identify support and resistance areas. And sometimes they can provide price objectives. But, for most investors, point and figure charts are best used as an additional investment tool to confirm or challenge other technical and fundamental work.

Technical Indicators Suppose a baseball player at bat happened to notice that almost every time a pitcher wiped his hand across his shirt the next pitch would be a fast ball. The batter might still strike out but, with this knowledge, he has a better chance for a hit. Analysts rely on technical indicators in much the same way. The use of these statistical tools as an aid in stock market timing is perhaps the most interesting and intellectually stimulating part of technical analysis.

There are literally hundreds of technical indicators. Most are derived from four primary sources:

- Business data
- Analysis of investor activity
- Market action
- Non-related coincidental factors

The indicators explained on the following pages have been fairly reliable in the past. Few, if any, work perfectly at every turn in the stock market. For this reason, an investor should maintain a portfolio of indicators or perhaps establish a composite index of several indicators.

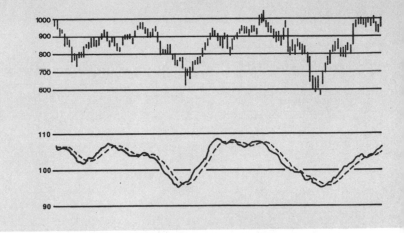

Dow Jones
Industrials

Money Supply
Indicator

Money Supply Indicator

Many Wall Street professionals believe there is a correlation between stock prices and the expansion or contraction of the nation's money supply. Indeed, a study of the thirty year period 1945-1975 suggests a definite correlation if inflation is also taken into account. When money supply is increasing at a fairly steady rate and inflation is low and of little concern, stock prices tend to rise. On the other hand, either a contraction of money supply growth or an increase in the rate of inflation or both can be considered an unfavorable development for the stock market.

The Money Supply Indicator is calculated monthly. It shows the year-to-year percent change in M_2 (defined by the Federal Reserve as currency plus demand deposits plus deposits at commercial banks other than large CD's) adjusted for the year-to-year percent change in the Consumer Price Index (CPI). To calculate the indicator, the percent change of M_2 and the inflation impact (as measured by the percent change of the CPI) are added to or subtracted from 100. For example, if, last month, M_2 increased 6.5% over the same month a year ago and the Consumer Price Index increased 4.0% in the same period, the Money Supply Indicator would read 102.5 for that

month (100 + 6.5 - 4.0). On the other hand, if M_2 advanced 3.0% while the CPI increased 5.8%, the Money Supply Indicator would only be 97.2 for the month (100 + 3.0 - 5.8).

In the late 1940's the Money Supply Indicator was frequently under 100 because the rate of inflation was greater than the growth of money supply. Corporate profits advanced but stocks remained dormant. Throughout most of the 1950's the indicator fluctuated in the 100-104 range. At that time the money supply increased modestly while the inflation rate remained low. Stock prices rose.

As the chart shows, stocks can be vulnerable when the indicator declines, but seem to do well when it is steady or rising. An investor should be especially cautious when the indicator is declining while stock prices are advancing. This happened in mid-1968 and early 1972. Conversely, if the indicator is rising sharply when stocks are declining, as it did in early 1970, the market could be nearing a turn for the better.

The Money Supply Indicator can be especially helpful during uncertain economic periods when money supply and inflation rate figures are in the limelight.

Index of 12 Leading Indicators

An economist with a sense of humor once said the stock market has correctly predicted eleven of the last nine economic recessions. While the market has a history of being volatile and does not always move in concert with the economy, it does have a reasonably good record of correctly forecasting the fortunes of American business.

Each month the Bureau of Economic Analysis of the U.S. Department of Commerce announces its Composite Index of 12 Leading Indicators which is regarded by many as the most important government index of the future state of the economy. Like the stock market, the Composite Index has been helpful but not perfect in predicting business conditions. Included among the twelve indicators is an index of stock prices. The other eleven indicators are the average workweek of manufacturing production workers, the manufacturing layoff rate, vendor performance, percent change in total liquid assets, percent change in sensitive prices, contracts and orders for plant and equipment, an index of net business formations, money balance (M_1), new orders, building permits and change in inventories.

This indicator is difficult to use because the government constantly revises the Index. However, it does have some value as a barometer of investor sentiment. Rightly or wrongly, the business community often thinks of the Index as a portent of things to come.

As a general rule, an investor should not be buying stocks aggressively when the Index appears to be in the initial stages of a decline — especially after many months of advancing. Conversely, when the Index begins to rise after a prolonged decline, it is best to avoid selling stocks short. However, in most other situations, the Index of Leading Indicators has limited value as a technical market tool.

Dow Jones Industrials

NYSE Short Interest Ratio

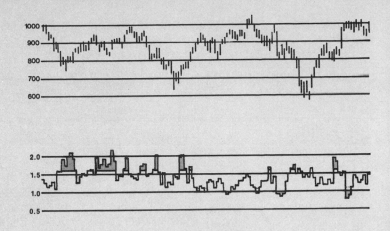

Short Interest Ratio

At about mid-month, the New York Stock Exchange announces its short interest. These are shares that have been borrowed and sold by investors who believe the same shares will be available later for repurchase at lower prices. Although a large short interest indicates many investors anticipate lower prices, it also represents potential buying power. In the past, NYSE short interest has been a reliable market indicator — especially when short sale figures have been related to the number of shares traded.

The "Short Interest Ratio" is a measure of this relationship. It is calculated by dividing the NYSE short interest total by the average daily NYSE volume over the same period. For example, if short interest totaled 24 million shares as of the middle of October and the daily volume from mid-September to mid-October averaged 20 million shares, the October short interest ratio would be 1.20 (i.e., 24,000,000 divided by 20,000,000).

When the average daily volume exceeds the short interest figure (i.e., a ratio of less than 1.00), the indicator reading is bearish. A short interest ratio of 1.00 to 1.60 is regarded as neutral and a ratio of more than 1.60 is bullish. It has generally been a good time to buy stocks when short interest has been at least double the average daily volume (when the ratio is 2.00 or more).

The short interest ratio has been a very popular and useful technical indicator. Like most other indicators, however, it is not infallible, as the chart illustrates.

Some technicians believe the short interest ratio will become distorted as more investors use stock options as an alternative method of selling short during a bear market. Others disagree by arguing that short selling could actually become more popular since options can be used to hedge short positions. Only time will tell.

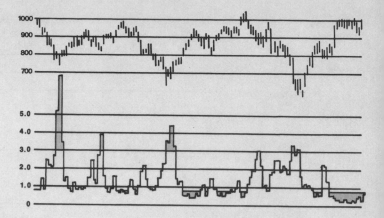

Dow Jones Industrials

1000 · 900 · 800 · 700

Odd Lot Short Sale Ratio

5.0 · 4.0 · 3.0 · 2.0 · 1.0 · 0

Odd Lot Short Sale Ratio

It is a widely accepted rule on Wall Street that the "odd lot" investor (defined as a buyer or seller of less than 100 shares), is almost always wrong. Yet, a close study of odd lot behavior does not bear this out entirely. The record clearly shows, for example, that odd lot investors were heavy net buyers at the market lows of 1966 and 1970 and were aggressive sellers at the highs in 1968 and 1972.

However, at moments of extreme optimism or pessimism, the odd lot investor can become emotional. One of the best barometers of this emotion is the Odd Lot Short Sale Ratio. This indicator has been particularly reliable at bear market lows.

The ratio is calculated by dividing odd lot short sales by total odd lot sales. These New York Stock Exchange statistics appear in many newspapers daily. The weekly totals, two weeks old but more complete, are summarized each Monday in the *Wall Street Journal* or *Barron's,* a weekly financial newspaper.

The chart above presents a ten year record of the Odd Lot Short Sale Ratio (calculated monthly by averaging the weekly figures). When the odd lot short sale ratio reaches or exceeds 3.0%, the indicator is considered positive. When the ratio declines to 0.7% or less, the reading is negative.

Stock options and anticipated changes within the overall market-making system might diminish the reliability of this technical indicator. For this reason, the investor should not rely on only one or two indicators.

Member Short Sales Ratio

Although two weeks old, the weekly New York Stock Exchange round lot statistics that appear in the *Wall Street Journal* and *Barron's* on Mondays constitute one of the most valuable technical indicators available. In addition to *total* shares purchased, sold and sold short, this weekly report also shows the number of shares purchased, sold and sold short for member accounts. The specialists, floor traders, and "off-the-floor" traders involved in trading for member accounts are among the most astute people on Wall Street. When member firms' short selling is high relative to total short sales, the "Member Short Sales Ratio," as it is called, is bearish. Conversely, when member shorts are proportionately less, the indicator is bullish.

The Member Short Sales Ratio is calculated weekly by dividing all shares sold short for member accounts by total short sales for the same period. The indicator is negative when member short selling is 82% or more of the total and is positive when the ratio is 68% or less.

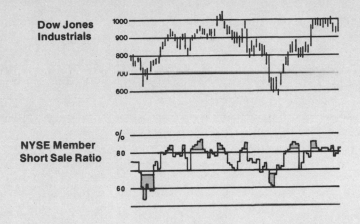

Dow Jones
Industrials

NYSE Member
Short Sale Ratio

Technical analysts also use the Specialists' Short Sale Ratio which is calculated in almost the same manner. However, this indicator has been somewhat less reliable than the overall member ratio because specialists are sometimes forced to go short. Traditionally, when specialists' short sales reach or exceed 60% of total short sales the ratio is bearish; when it drops to 40% or less it is considered bullish.

The chart above shows a seven year record of the weekly Member Short Sales Ratio averaged monthly.

Other Technical Observations The use of indicators in technical analysis is limited only by one's imagination. Here are several other ideas technicians use:

- Market breadth studies. These are based on various interpretations of cumulative advances and declines on the NYSE.
- Customers' margin debt on the New York Stock Exchange. A rising margin debt is considered positive; a declining margin debt is negative.
- Studies based on the inverse relationship between commercial paper rates and stock prices.
- Numerous studies of relationships between stock prices and volume.

- The total market value of New York Stock Exchange stocks as a percent of the nation's Gross National Product. In the past, a ratio below 40% has been positive, above 70% has been negative.
- An analysis of personal buying and selling activity by company executives. These figures are reported to the S.E.C. and are worth noting when three or more officers buy within a month of each other while none sells. The same rule applies to "insiders" who sell.
- The market value of $1 of dividends (the inverse to stock yields). Using the Dow Jones Industrial Average as a benchmark, the market has been fully valued at or above 30 times each dollar of dividends and at attractive levels at or below 15 times.
- The cash holdings of mutual funds as a percent of total fund assets. A 10% level or higher is thought to be positive while a 6% level or below is considered to be unfavorable.

The statistical sources for these and most other technical indicators are plentiful. Local libraries, for instance, offer a variety of publications with business and economic data. Once all past figures have been collected, keeping the indicators current is an easy task.

Many market analysts are convinced there are other, unexplained forces that influence stock prices. For example, over the years there have been distinct seasonal trends. The best months for rising prices traditionally have been January, July, November and December. The worst months have been February, May, June and October. This explains why buyers in May and June hope to see a "summer rally" and why October buyers look forward to the so-called "year end rally."

Short term traders with years of experience are aware that, on balance, Mondays have been "down" days while Fridays have been "up" days. Also, when the market declines on Friday, there seems to be a strong tendency for prices to decline further on Monday.

Are there stock market cycles? Some analysts think so. It is interesting to note that, with the exception of only one instance (1930), each fourth year since 1914 provided an excellent time to buy stocks:

1914	1930	1946	1962
1918	1934	1950	1966
1922	1938	1954	1970
1926	1942	1958	1974

Moreover, every "5 year" since 1905 has been a year of rising stock prices (1915, 1925, 1935, 1945, 1955, 1965 and 1975).

One other force not to be overlooked is "market psychology." The emotions and herd instincts that once possessed entire populations during the Tulip Craze, the Mississippi Scheme and the South Sea Bubble were described more than one hundred years ago by Charles Mackay in his classic book, *Extraordinary Popular Delusions and the Madness of Crowds*. Today, circumstances may have changed, but human nature remains the same.

The force of market psychology may never be understood, much less predicted, but the technical analyst is a step closer to harnessing it.

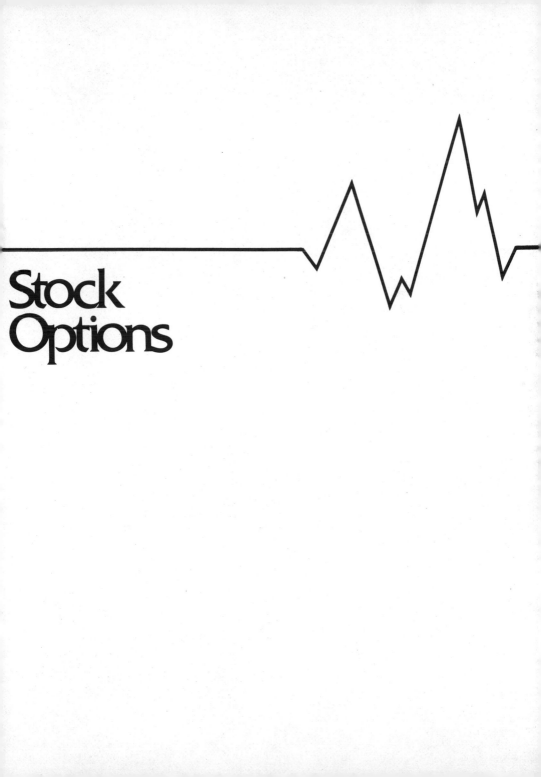

Stock
Options

Introduction Since April 26, 1973, when the Chicago Board Options Exchange (CBOE) revolutionized trading in stock options, the growth of the options market has been explosive.

The average daily contract volume on the CBOE was close to 10,000 contracts in 1973. Now, ten times that amount is not unusual. Dollar volume, based on the prices paid for options, has increased from $448 million in 1973 to a multi-billion dollar business today.

Options had suddenly been discovered even though they had been trading quietly in the Over-The-Counter market for at least 100 years. Some hailed them as the new way to quick profits in any type of market while others dismissed them abruptly as just another form of outright gambling. As they become more widely understood, however, options will undoubtedly be recognized for what they are — an additional investment tool for knowledgeable investors and seasoned speculators.

The mechanics of put and call options, suggestions for valuing them and methods for using them are among the highlights of this chapter.

174

Background A stock option is a contract that gives the owner the right to buy or sell a specific number of shares (usually 100) of a given stock at a fixed price within a definite time period. The stock involved is referred to as the "underlying security," the fixed price is called the "striking price" or "strike price" and the date the contract expires is called the "expiration date." For the privileges of the option, the buyer pays a "premium," another name for the option's "price." It is not a down payment and it must be paid in full in cash. The premium is the only variable in any option contract; all other items are fixed. And, like the price of a common stock, the premium is an equilibrium price reflecting the judgments of all buyers and sellers in the market at any given time.

An option conveying the right to *buy* stock from the option's seller (the "writer") is known as a "call" because it allows the buyer to call stock away from the writer. An option conveying the right to *sell* stock to the writer is termed a "put" because it allows the buyer to put stock to the writer. Either action by the buyer is known as "exercising" the option. Once an option has been written, the writer must abide by its stated terms. However, the writer can extinguish this responsibility, as explained later.

Stock options are currently traded on most of the national exchanges including the Chicago Board Options Exchange, presently the leader in options activity. All are regulated by the Securities and Exchange Commission. Each day's trading results on each exchange is summarized in the *Wall Street Journal* and several other major daily newspapers. The excerpt from a typical options table illustrated on the next page explains some option market terminology. These tables present price and volume information from the previous trading session for each class of options as well as the closing prices of the underlying stocks. A "class" is composed of all options, both puts and calls, covering the same underlying security. Thus, all Sears options constitute a class.

Three expiration dates are given for each strike price. The illustration shows the Sears call options of July, October and January of the new year. If these were put options, the table would be identical but a "p" would appear immediately after the name of the underlying security. Under current practices of the exchanges, expiration dates are spaced in three month intervals extending out to nine months, the most distant expiration date now available. When the July "series" expire, trading will begin in the

The Exchange where the options are traded. Options on the same stock can be available on more than one exchange.

The Expiration Date. Options expire on the Saturday immediately following the third Friday of the month. Thus, the third Friday is the last trading day.

Chicago Board

Option &	price	— Jul — Vol.	Last	— Oct — Vol.	Last	— Jan — Vol.	Last	N.Y. Close
Nw Air	25	69	1 11-16	130	2⅜	a	a	26
Nw Air	.30	111	¼	18	9-16	18	1 3-16	26
Pennz	...25	10	6	b	b	b	b	32⅜
Pennz	.. 30	229	2⅝	33	3⅜	37	3¾	32⅜
Pennz	..35	399	¼	85	1⅛	60	1¼	32⅜
Pepsi	.. 70	12	3	1	4½	a	a	70¾
Pepsi	.. 80	39	⅜	13	1 5-16	a	a	70¾
Polar	...30	508	4⅜	34	5⅛	38	5⅝	33⅝
Polar	...35	742	1⅜	367	2 5-16	107	3	33⅝
Polar	.. 40	146	3-16	330	13-16	b	b	33⅝
R C A	..20	10	10	b	b	b	b	29⅞
R C A	..25	104	5⅛	19	5⅝	36	6	29⅞
R C A	..30	703	1⅜	194	2	92	2 7-16	29⅞
Sears	..50	212	7⅝	2	8¼	1	8⅝	57¾
Sears	..60	203	1⅛	64	2 3-16	28	3	57¾
Sears	70	25	⅛	a	a	b	b	57¾
Sperry	..35	70	1⅝	82	2 7-16	62	3⅛	34⅞
Sperry	..40	62	¼	54	⅝	124	1⅛	34⅞
Sperry	..45	2	1-16	b	b	b	b	34⅞
Syntex	..15	4	3	2	3⅛	3	3⅞	17¾
Syntex	..20	161	⅜	76	13-16	32	1¼	17¾
Syntex	..25	47	⅛	9	3-16	b	b	17¾

a-Not traded. b-No option offered.
Sales in 100s. Last is premium (purchase price).

Volume indicates the number of option contracts traded.

The Underlying Security. Each option typically represents 100 shares of the underlying security.

The Premium is the market price of the option.

The Closing Price of the underlying security on the New York Stock Exchange.

The "Strike" Price. The option buyer acquires stock from the option writer at this price if the buyer exercises a *call* option. The option buyer sells stock to the writer at this price if the buyer exercises a *put* option.

In June, 1981, the *Journal* and other major newspapers changed the options table format. However, the information is essentially the same as explained above. An example of the new format is shown on the right.

Chicago Board

Option & NY Close	Strike Price	Calls—Last Aug	Nov	Feb	Puts—Last Aug	Nov	Feb
Hewlet	.. 70	a	b	b	⅛	b	b
99¼	80	21	a	b	½	1⅛	b
99¼	... 90	12½	17½	a	1½	2¾	3½
99¼	.. 100	6¼	10½	13½	4⅝	6⅞	9
99¼	.. 110	2⅛	6¼	10	11	12	a
H Inns	.. 20	12¾	a	b	a	a	b
32	25	7⅝	8½	9⅛	1-16	a	a
32	 30	3¼	4¼	5⅛	9-16	1 1-16	1½
32	35	⅞	2	2⅞	a	a	a
Honwll	.. 80	6	8¾	11	1⅞	3⅛	4⅜
82	 90	1 13-16	4½	7½	7⅝	8⅛	8½
82	 100	⅜	1¾	3¼	17⅜	17¾	17
82	110	1-16	11-16	b	b	b	b
82	120	1-16	b	b	b	b	b
82	110	b	b	b	27⅝	25¾	b
In Flv	... 20	2¾	3½	a	b	b	b
22¼	25	⅜	⅞	1½	b	b	b
J Manv	..20	1¾	2¾	a	⅝	1	1⅛
20⅝	25	5-16	¾	1¼	a	a	a
20⅝	... 30	1-16	a	b	a	a	b
Mobil	50	6⅜	8⅞	9¾	7-16	1 1-16	1 9-16
55⅝	... 55	3¼	5¼	7	2	2⅝	3¼
55⅝	... 60	1¼	3	4⅝	5	5¾	5¾
55⅝	... 65	⅜	1½	2¾	9⅞	10	10
55⅝	70	3-16	¾	b	14⅞	a	b
55⅝	80	1-16	5-16	b	24⅝	a	b

new April series and the option tables in newspapers will be amended to show October, January and April expiration dates. Depending upon the exchange and, of course, the time of the year, the option tables also show other consecutive series combinations.

New strike prices are introduced when the price of the underlying stock advances or declines. This will usually occur at five point intervals for stocks trading below $50 a share; ten point intervals for stocks trading between $50 and $200 a share and twenty point intervals for stocks trading above $200 a share. For instance, if Sears common stock, last traded on the NYSE at 57⅜ as shown in the column on the far right, were suddenly to advance to about $70, new options would probably be established with a strike price of $80 for all or some of the given expiration dates. Options with a new $45 strike price would probably be introduced if the stock were to fall below $50.

At times, however, no options are offered at an existing strike price under a given expiration date. This would be noted by the letter "b" in the tables. Thus, there are no Sears January 70 Calls being offered. In general, new options are introduced as the expiration date changes or when the market price changes enough to war-

rant a new strike price. The letter "a" in the tables means that options are available but that none was traded that day.

Each line, then, summarizes the previous trading day's statistics for the options in each series. The interested options investor learns, for example, that the last trade of a Sears July 50 Call took place at a premium of $7.625 per share of the underlying stock. Since each option contract covers 100 shares of the underlying stock, the premium listed in the table must be multiplied by 100 to compute the actual dollar cost of a single option of any series. In this case, the premium would be $762.50 for one Sears July 50 Call. Similarly, the figure in the volume column indicates that 212 individual July 50 Call contracts were bought and sold representing 21,200 shares of the underlying stock. To repeat, in every instance, the figures would have the same meaning if puts were being discussed rather than calls.

Today's market contrasts sharply with the early days of options trading. In the 1920's, for example, most options activity took place in a small restaurant on New Street in New York's financial district. Each day a small cadre of options traders turned the restaurant into their own office, dining room, and after hours club. They arrived early and set up shop near the public telephone booths. Their pockets jingled with change for what was then a nickel telephone call. Some of the more prosperous brokers employed messengers who crisscrossed the Wall Street area trying to bring buyers and sellers together. However, matching the buyer and writer was usually difficult and often impossible. It was a process that invariably required several telephone calls and exasperating negotiation to formulate terms agreeable to both the buyer and the writer. If an options investor decided the contract was no longer useful, it was even more difficult to sell it to someone else in a secondary market. The CBOE rejuvenated options trading when it standardized the terms of an option contract and when it created a central marketplace.

The trading floor of the CBOE was built in the air-space above the trading pits used by the commodities exchange. In this old section, a similar type of options trading has long been practiced in contracts for wheat, soybeans, potatoes and other commodities.

There are currently eleven oval trading counters on the floor of the CBOE. Options on several underlying stocks are traded at each counter. The traders group outside the counters watching each other for out-crys of interest as well as the television set

display units above each counter. Up-to-the-minute pricing information on each option traded at the counter appears on the display units. The data includes the last premium trade, the current bid and asked quotation and the underlying stock's trading information. When a trade is completed among the floor traders, the results are quickly passed to CBOE employees working inside the counter and the new trading information immediately appears on the screens above. Much of this data is also available on the electronic quotation machines used in brokerage firms throughout the country. Representatives of the various member brokerage firms are stationed at communications booths that ring the trading floor. Messengers carry orders from the communication booths to the floor traders, and soon return with the completed trade information. In this way, the firm's customers quickly learn the results of each transaction.

The Options Clearing Corporation serves as a giant bookkeeping operation recording the actions of all buyers and sellers. After the orders are matched on the trading floor, the Clearing Corporation acts as the buyer to every seller and the seller to every buyer. It severs the relationship between the original writer and the original buyer. This combination of the Clearing Corpora-

THE OPTIONS CLEARING CORPORATION

OPTION CERTIFICATE

C 00448

THE UNDERSIGNED, THE OPTIONS CLEARING CORPORATION (THE "CORPORATION"),

HEREBY CERTIFIES THAT   VOID CERTIFICATE: TO BE USED AS SAMPLE

(THE CLEARING MEMBER) IS THE HOLDER OF THE FOLLOWING EXCHANGE TRADED OPTION CONTRACT (S):

THE AFORESAID OPTION CONTRACT(S) MAY BE EXERCISED OR CLOSED OUT THROUGH THE CLEARING MEMBER IN A CLOSING WRITING TRANSACTION ON A PARTICIPATING EXCHANGE OF THE CORPORATION ONLY IN ACCORDANCE WITH THE THEN APPLICABLE BY-LAWS, RULES AND PROCEDURES OF THE CORPORATION AND ONLY UPON THE SURRENDER TO THE CORPORATION OF THIS OPTION CERTIFICATE. THIS OPTION CERTIFICATE IS A NON-NEGOTIABLE INSTRUMENT, AND THE TRANSFER HEREOF DOES NOT CHANGE THE OWNERSHIP OF THE AFORESAID OPTION CONTRACT(S) EXCEPT WITH THE CONSENT OF THE CORPORATION.

THE OPTIONS CLEARING CORPORATION

Options certificates are not widely used but they are available.

tion and the active secondary market makes it possible for an option owner to sell at any time and for an option writer to terminate the responsibility to deliver or accept stock at any time. The owner of an option instructs the broker to sell it in much the same manner as a common stock would be sold. This action is called a "closing sale transaction." The writer terminates the responsibility to deliver or accept stock through a "closing purchase transaction," also called "buying-in." In this transaction, the writer buys an option identical in all respects to the option originally written except for the premium. The outstanding option is then offset at the Clearing Corporation with the option purchased in the closing purchase transaction. In each case, the profit or loss of either the writer or the buyer is determined by the difference between the original premium paid or received and the premium paid or received in the closing transaction. If only one investor liquidates a position as writer or buyer, it has no effect on the other investor. That is, if a call writer liquidates a position in a closing transaction, the owner of the call may still exercise it at any time.

Buying Options For buyers, options offer leverage with a predetermined risk. The option's cost is its premium and this premium is usually only a small fraction of the underlying stock's market price. Thus, the buyer participates in any price change in the stock without having to buy the stock itself which would require a substantially greater investment. Further, the buyer knows that the maximum possible loss is the total amount of the premium.

In practice, most option buyers expect to profit from an increase in the premium. They are not interested in exercising the option to acquire the stock itself but are attracted by capital gains leverage and limited capital exposure.

Here is a simplified explanation of how an option buyer can make or lose money on an option trade . . .

After studying the fundamental and technical characteristics of the ABC Company, an investor concludes in late April that the company's common stock price will increase substantially in the next three months. The stock is selling for $40 a share.

	Stock			**Call Option**	
April	Bought 100 shares @ $40	$4,000		Bought 1 July 40 Call @ $4	$ 400
June	Sold 100 shares @ $46	4,600		Sold 1 July 40 Call @ $7	700
	Trading Profit	$ 600		Trading Profit	$ 300
	Less approximate commissions	135		Less approximate commissions	50
	PROFIT	$ 465		PROFIT	$ 250
	Net Return on Original Investment Before Taxes	11.6%		Net Return on Original Investment Before Taxes	62.5%

The investor could either buy the stock outright or buy a call on the stock. Since the stock purchase would require an immediate outlay of $4,000 — excluding commissions — for 100 shares, the investor decides to take advantage of the inherent leverage of options. A July ABC 40 Call is purchased for a premium of 4 ($400 for 100 shares). The July expiration date was selected because, as the investor reasoned, the underlying stock would advance soon. By late June, the stock price increased 15% to $46 while the option advanced to 7, a gain of 75%. At this point, the investor may want to sell the option in the secondary market to capture the 3 point increase in the premium. The comparison above shows how an investor would profit by either owning the stock directly or by buying a call.

The absolute dollar profit was less from the call option than from the stock but, compared to the capital invested, the call option produced a greater profit.

If the stock's potential had been misjudged and it declined rather than advanced, the maximum loss would be the entire initial premium of $400. The stock could drop by more than the premium amount but the call buyer's loss is still limited to $400. Although the buyer might be able to reduce this loss by selling the call in the secondary market for whatever value remained, any loss to the call owner is an immediate out-of-pocket cash loss. On the other hand, the owner of stock only has a "paper loss" and can hold the shares for future recovery.

Assuming in this example the investor expected the stock's price to drop sharply in the same short time period, the premium of a July ABC 40 Put would have increased in value as the underlying stock declined. Puts are calls turned upside down. And, like calls, puts offer leverage and limited loss of capital but in reverse. Puts are appropriate in a declining market as opposed to the traditional method of profiting from falling stock prices by selling stock short. Stated differently, a put option is to a short sale as a call option is to buying the stock "long."

Under current margin requirements of 50%, selling short 100 shares of ABC at $40 in late April, would have required a margin deposit of at least $2,000. If, two months later, the stock dropped 15% to $34 as expected, the investor would have had a profit of $600 or 30%.

The purchase of an ABC July 40 Put in late April at 4 would have produced a 75% profit in the same period if the premium had advanced to 7 as the stock declined — excluding commissions and taxes.

The put limited the buyer's potential loss to the amount of the premium while the short seller's risk was theoretically unlimited. Moreover, puts give an options investor greater psychological staying power. For example, if the stock had advanced before it began the anticipated decline, the short seller might have been tempted to cover prematurely. The put buyer, on the other hand, realizing that the total possible loss was limited to $400, could have endured the advance more easily.

It should be noted, however, that if the stock remained steady and did not decline to $34 until August, the short seller would still have made a 30% profit while the put would have expired worthless.

Writing Options Option sellers are called "writers" in a carryover from the early days of Over-The-Counter trading when the details of each contract had to be carefully written out by hand. Today, option writing is standardized but the term remains.

An option writer's primary purpose is to earn additional income through the premiums received from option buyers. This income can sometimes add to the overall return on a given portfolio. Premium income can also provide a "cushion" against an adverse move in the underlying stock — but only to the extent of the premium.

Assume an investor who owns CDE Company stock at a cost of $50 writes a CDE 50 Call and receives a premium of $5. If the stock does not move and the option expires worthless, the entire 5 point premium can be considered additional income. If the stock advances, it can be called away, which means the investor is, in effect, selling the stock for $55. The writer's maximum profit is, therefore, limited to the premium amount.

The premium also hedges the stock against a decline to $45. If the stock drops by more than the premium, the investor will suffer a loss. Obviously, writing covered calls increases the total rate of return on a given

Display units present option prices on the floor of the American Stock Exchange.

181

portfolio only if the underlying stock neither increases nor decreases by more than the amount of the premium.

While all option purchases require a full cash payment, option writing involves more complex accounting. Most writing takes place in a margin account. The options written may be "covered" or "uncovered" (also called "naked"). A call is covered most simply if the writer deposits with the broker the exact number of shares of underlying stock to be sold if the option is exercised. A covered call writer can choose between delivering the stock on deposit or delivering stock bought in the open market when the option was exercised. Some writers who have a low cost on the stock already owned may select the latter method to avoid paying a large capital gains tax at that time.

A naked call (a call written against cash) can only be written in a margin account. A broker requires that adequate funds be on hand at all times to purchase stock in the open market if the option is exercised. A put is covered only when it is offset share for share by a long put having an equal or greater exercise price. The margin requirements for writing uncovered puts and calls are identical. Whenever a margin account is used, the investor should compute the transaction's ultimate rate of return based on the amount of capital deposited.

Naked call writing has much greater risk than covered call writing. If the stock either remains steady or declines, naked calls can produce large returns on the margin deposited. But if it advances, every point beyond the amount of premium initially received will be an out-of-pocket loss to the writer when the call is exercised. The naked call writer, like the investor who sells stock short, could have unlimited losses.

Some option investors, eager to increase their premium income, mix covered and naked calls in a strategy known as "variable hedging." The variable hedger writes more than one option for each 100 shares owned. For example, an investor who owns 100 shares of EFG Company at $40 writes three EFG 40 Calls for a premium of $4 each or a total premium income of $12. By definition, one call is covered and two are naked. The $12 premium could offset a substantial decline in the stock owned to $28. However, if the stock were to rise, each 1 point advance beyond $46 would increase the variable hedger's loss by $2 until the calls are finally exercised. At $46, the $12 premium offsets the $6 increased cost for each share of stock underlying each of the naked calls.

The variable hedge, then, has two break-even points and at any price between them, the hedger will make a profit. In this example, the two points were $28 on the downside and $46 on the upside. Each additional option written extends the downside breakeven point but lowers the upside breakeven point. The investor receives greater premium income but is also exposed to the substantial risk inherent in writing naked calls. This risk combined with the difficulty of predicting short term price changes makes writing naked calls hard to justify. Even if it appears certain that the stock will collapse, writing naked calls is not the best method of exploiting the anticipated decline. Either shorting the stock outright or buying a put will produce greater profits from a steep price drop because the writer's maximum profit is always limited to the premium.

All writers can buy-in the option at any time rather than wait for the expiration date. For example, a covered GHI Company $50 Call has been written for a $5 premium. The underlying stock, that the writer owns at $50 a share, advances to $55 and the premium advances to 7. If the stock appears to be headed higher, the writer could buy-in the option at 7. This closing purchase transaction would produce a $2 loss on the option trade, but would leave a $5 unrealized gain in the stock with the potential for greater profits if it continues to advance as expected.

Put writers, like call writers, hope the premiums they receive will mean additional income. Since put writers buy stock rather than sell stock, the contracts they write are not covered by stock as they are with call writers. Although it is possible to write covered puts as mentioned earlier, most puts are uncovered and are written against cash. Actually, if a put and a call have identical premiums, exercise prices and expiration dates, the covered call writer and the uncovered put writer will have the same maximum dollar risk and reward after the options are written. If the options are exercised, the premium a put writer receives reduces the purchase cost of the stock just as the premium from writing a covered call is part of the proceeds of the sale.

Put writing, like call writing, also finds its greatest utility when the underlying stock neither increases nor decreases by more than the amount of the premium.

XYZ Calls at 40 Strike Price	**XYZ Puts at 40 Strike Price**
Stock Price	*Stock Price*

	Stock Price	Stock Price
In-the-money	Over 40	Under 40
At-the-money	40	40
Out-of-the-money	Under 40	Over 40

Premium Valuation At any given moment, the amount of an option's premium is a function of the following:

(1) The relationship or expected relationship between the current price of the underlying stock and the option's strike price.

(2) The amount of time remaining before the expiration date.

(3) The volatility of the underlying stock.

(4) The dividend of the underlying stock.

(5) The level and direction of short-term interest rates.

These factors are built into the premiums of all options and if they change, the level of the premiums will also change.

In practice, once the underlying stock and its probable direction have been identified, there is still the problem of selecting one option out of the many available to obtain the best combination of risk and reward. To do this, the option buyer must begin by answering two questions:

(1) What is the extent of the stock's expected move?

(2) In what time period will the stock make its expected move?

Stated simply, option premiums in the same class are two-dimensional. There is a *vertical dimension* involving the stock price/strike price relationship and a *horizontal dimension* involving time. By answering the two questions, the options investor will be better equipped to cope with these two dimensions.

The Vertical Dimension

The relationship of the stock price to the strike price determines whether an option is "in-the-money," "at-the-money" or "out-of-the-money" as the table above illustrates.

A call is out-of-the-money when the stock price is below the strike price, at-the-money when the stock price and the strike price are the same and in-the-money when the stock price is above the strike price. Puts are described with the same terms but in reverse.

An in-the-money call option is said to have "intrinsic value" by the amount the underlying stock is above the strike price. Thus, in the example above, with the stock selling at $44, a call option's intrinsic value would be $4. The term "intrinsic value" is used to denote the value that can be captured immediately by exercising the option and selling the stock.

Just as intrinsic value is included when evaluating premiums of in-the-money options, this book is introducing the term "price concession" for out-of-the-money options. Price concession is the opposite of intrinsic value. It is the amount by which the stock is below the strike price. A call with a $40 strike price would have a price concession of $2 when the stock is $38. Neither intrinsic value nor price concession are fixed values. Their amounts depend upon the current price of the underlying stock and thus will change as the stock's price changes. Both terms "intrinsic value" and "price concession" also apply to put options but, again, in reverse.

Unfortunately, intrinsic value and price concession do not entirely explain this vertical dimension. The investor who buys a call option for $5 when the stock is selling $3 above its strike price is paying $2 above the intrinsic value of the premium. This $2 is the cost of the time remaining in the contract. In other words, the difference between the premium and its intrinsic value is its "time cost." Time becomes less important as the stock price moves higher and as the intrinsic value increases. Conversely, when the stock price declines below the strike price, the premium is purely time cost since the option has no intrinsic value. Although, on the surface,

the premium appears low, there is a hidden time cost (the price concession). Unlike intrinsic value when the option is in-the-money, price concession is not included in the premium. Even though price concession is only a theoretical time cost and not a "real" time cost, it should not be ignored.

The table at the top of the next page shows there is less risk and less reward for the XYZ Call buyer the further the stock price is above the strike price. It also shows greater risk and greater reward the further the stock price is below the strike price. As the option acquires intrinsic value, it loses leverage. The relatively larger premium reduces the option's sensitivity to further increases in the price of the underlying stock (i.e., the option's reward). At the same time, the presence of intrinsic value also reduces risk.

Similarly, as price concession increases, risk also increases because the probability of the option ever attaining intrinsic value decreases. The reward potential is also increasing because a small premium investment could produce dramatic gains if the stock were to advance substantially.

The further the stock is from the strike price, either up or down, the more the stock must move to justify the option investment. And the probability of a stock moving, say, 10% in the course of a few months is much

			XYZ Company Call Option @ 40				
Stock Price	Price Concession	Intrinsic Value	Premium	% of Stock Price	Time Cost	% of Stock Price
52	—	12.00	13.375	25.7%	1.375	2.6%
50	—	10.00	11.75	23.5	1.75	3.5
48	—	8.00	10.00	20.8	2.00	4.2
46	—	6.00	8.125	17.7	2.125	4.6
44	—	4.00	6.375	14.5	2.375	5.4
42	—	2.00	4.50	10.7	2.50	6.0
Strike Price 40	—	—	3.25	8.1	3.25*	8.1
38	2.00	—	1.75	4.6	3.75	9.9
36	4.00	—	1.125	3.1	5.125	14.2
34	6.00	—	0.50	1.5	6.50	19.1
32	8.00	—	0.25	0.8	8.25	25.8
30	10.00	—	0.125	0.4	10.125	33.8
28	12.00	—	0.06	0.2	12.06	43.1

*The greatest amount of "real" time cost.

greater than the probability of it moving 30% in the same time period.

For these reasons, the buyer should choose an option that provides the best combination of a low premium and a low time cost as a percentage of the underlying stock's price. As the table suggests, the most favorable cost combination is generally found in a narrow band slightly above and slightly below the strike price.

The charts on the following page show the first three months of trading of the International Business Machines (IBM) July 260's and July 280's from October, 1976 through January, 1977. Throughout this period the July 260's were consistently in-the-money and the July 280's were consistently out-of-the-money. In these early months the percentage moves of the July 280's were greater than the July 260's. With both options having, or nearly having, intrinsic value, investors turned their interest to the option with the lower premium because they could participate in the stock's move for less money.

How far out-of-the-money should an option buyer go to obtain greater reward? The answer depends on the extent of the stock's expected move. Investors might not recognize an option's potential for attaining intrinsic value until the stock has moved closer to the strike price. In the meantime, other options in its class with strike prices closer to the stock price have outperformed it. This also explains why a stock's volatility is an important consideration in the valuation of option premiums.

The fate of an expiring out-of-the-money option can be seen by comparing the charts showing the expirations of the IBM January 280's and the IBM January 260's. The stock price was $275 when both expired in January, 1977.

The Horizontal Dimension

An option is a "wasting asset" because the time remaining up to the expiration date has a value that diminishes day-by-day. Clearly, an XYZ option with an expiration date only two weeks away is worth less (and should have a smaller premium) than another XYZ option with the same strike price but not expiring for six months.

It has been shown that a premium includes a time cost that varies according to the stock price/strike price relationship. This time cost also varies according to the time remaining. Hence, the horizontal dimension. For this reason, it is necessary to ask "In what time period will the stock make its expected move?"

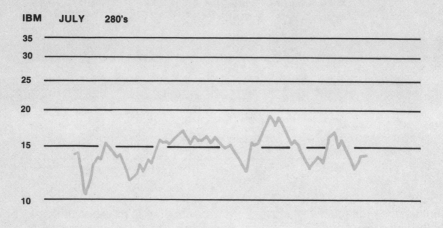

IBM   JULY   280's

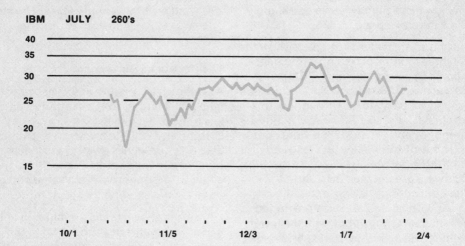

IBM   JULY   260's

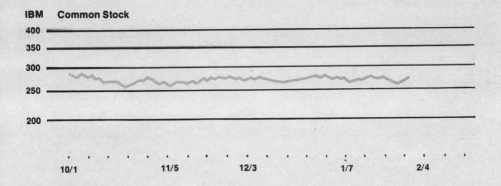

IBM Common Stock

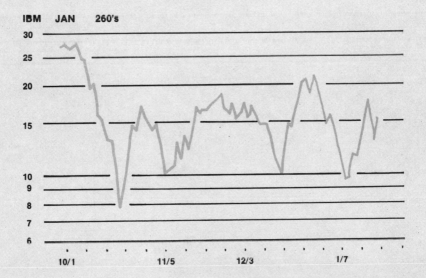

IBM JAN 260's

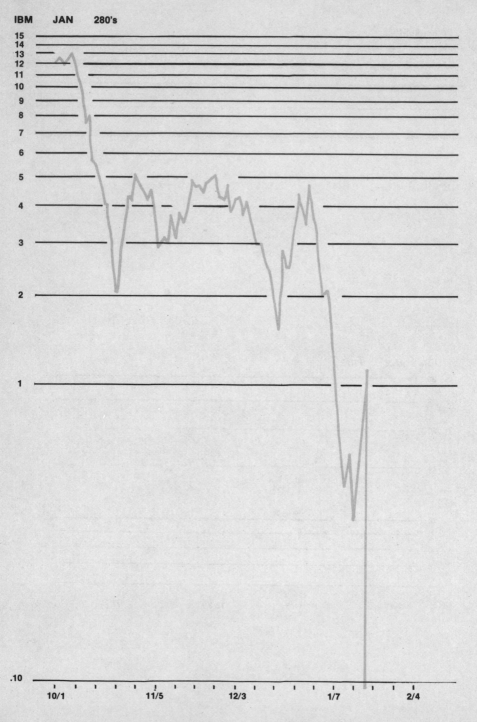

IBM   JAN   280's

The value of time can be seen by comparing the previous charts showing the early months of the IBM July 260's and the last few months of the January 260's. They traded side by side briefly in late 1976 and early 1977. Each had the same strike price and the same intrinsic value or price concession at any given moment, but the premium of the July 260's was consistently $10 or more above the January 260's. Understandably, the January option was also much more sensitive to the stock's price swings.

Now, using the vertical and horizontal dimension concept, the investor can compare all options in the same class.

Consider the following example . . .

On November 10, 1976, the common stock of Exxon Corporation closed on the New York Stock Exchange at 47¾. An interested investor, believing the end of the stock's decline was near, glanced at the option tables in the newspaper. The following calls were available on the CBOE:

	January	April	July
EXXON 45	3⅝	b	b
EXXON 50	1⅛	2⅛	2⅝
EXXON 55	¼	¾	b
EXXON 60	a	¼	¾

The investor reasoned that the stock price would rebound 10-15% within the next two or three months. The analysis proved correct, but which option produced the maximum gain?

On January 4, 1977, Exxon closed at 53⅝, up 12% in two months, and the Exxon call premiums closed as follows:

	January	April	July
EXXON 45	8¾	a	a
EXXON 50	3⅞	4⅞	5½
EXXON 55	⁷⁄₁₆	1¹¹⁄₁₆	b
EXXON 60	a	⁵⁄₁₆	⅞

From November to January, the Exxon calls increased by the percentages indicated below:

	January	April	July
EXXON 45	141%	—	—
EXXON 50	244%	129%	110%
EXXON 55	75%	125%	—
EXXON 60	—	25%	17%

The best results would have been obtained by purchasing the Exxon January 50's — the option with the strike price just above the stock price and with the shortest time period.

Many seasoned option buyers carry this idea a step further in a process called "walking up" an option. After the largest part of the premium's advance has been captured, the option is sold and the initial process is repeated over again. If the Exxon investor, for example, expected the stock to continue its advance by another 10-15% in the January-April period, the January 50 Calls would be replaced by the April 55 Calls, available on January 4 for $1\frac{11}{16}$. The investor would hold the option until the stock was no longer expected to increase or until the stock crossed above the strike price allowing the investor to walk up again.

This example enjoyed the benefit of 20-20 hindsight. In practice, correctly predicting a stock's short term price change is considerably more difficult, often impossible. In fact, had the Exxon investor bought the April 55's, the outcome would have been disappointing.

Option buyers will find it easier to compare premiums than to value them on an absolute basis. While there are numerous sophisticated formulas and theories designed to compute theoretical premium values, even the professional floor traders and market makers of the leading options exchanges temper theoretical values with their trading senses. Option buyers know how much can be lost but cannot say exactly how much might be made.

Writers are in a somewhat better position to make value judgments because the premium received can be considered an investment return to be compared with other available short-term opportunities. Option writers know how much can be made but cannot say exactly how much might be lost.

The premium a writer receives is basically compensation for:
(1) accepting the risk that the underlying stock could move adversely prior to the expiration date; and,
(2) agreeing to support the option written with a reserve of either stock or cash during the option's life.

The premium compensation, expressed as an annual rate of return on the capital invested, will obviously be subject to change as the market environment changes. When interest rates rise and alternative investment opportunities become more attractive, a writer should either expect a greater return or consider placing the capital elsewhere. And the reverse is true when interest rates and other investment returns are declining.

There is significantly greater risk in writing an option than in buying a Treasury Bill, for example. Clearly, an option writer should demand significantly greater compensation. But whether the compensation must be double the Treasury Bill rate or triple it before an investor is motivated to write options will depend on that investor's perception of the risks and rewards involved. Some investors will simply write options for a smaller return than will others.

Since option prices are equilibrium prices, a potential writer can quickly calculate what other option writers are demanding and buyers paying by reviewing the daily option quotations.

A writer, like a buyer, is usually faced with several strike prices and expiration dates. From these choices, the writer must select the option offering the best combination of risk and reward. For writers, as for buyers, this combination will most likely be found in the option that has a strike price slightly above or slightly below the current price of the underlying stock because, within this band, the writer will obtain the largest amount of "real" time cost.

The importance of real time cost is most evident when a covered call is written. In this instance, the writer's only possible net profit is, in fact, the amount of real time cost. For example, an investor buys IJK Company stock at $60 and, attracted by the large premium, writes an IJK 50 Call for $12. If the option is immediately exercised, the writer will deliver stock at $50. The $10 loss in the stock will be offset by the premium's $10 of intrinsic value. The writer's profit will be $2, or the premium's "real" time cost. If the stock had dropped to $50 and the option expired worthless, the net profit would also be $2. Of course, if the stock dropped by more than the total premium, the covered writer has a loss.

A writer's risk and reward combinations are the reverse of a buyer's: the more in-the-money the option is when it is written, the greater the risk and reward; the more out-of-the-money, the less risk and reward.

The Tax Reform Act of 1976 made important changes in the Internal Revenue Code which affect writers and other option investors. For example, items previously considered ordinary income are now regarded as capital transactions. The combined impact of new and pre-existing tax laws on the economics of any options trade should be carefully reviewed by every options investor with an accountant or tax advisor.

Reducing Risk One of the major attractions of options is their versatility. They can be used individually or combined in various ways to create strategies that modify an investor's risk/reward ratio. Many of these strategies are based directly on the relationships presented earlier. One very popular approach, called "spreading," involves the simultaneous purchase and sale of options on the same underlying stock. Of the numerous spreads available, two are frequently used in option investing: the *vertical spread* and the *calendar spread.*

The Vertical Spread

A vertical spread is formed by simultaneously buying (going long) and writing (going short) options on the same underlying stock with identical expiration dates but different strike prices. In a calendar spread, the options used have the same strike price but different expiration dates.

A premium is paid going long and a premium is received going short. Spreading takes its name from the "spread" or numerical difference between the two premiums. If the investor pays more than is received, the difference is called a "debit" and the investor is said to have "bought" the spread. A spread is "sold" with a "credit" if the premium received is greater than the premium paid. For example, a vertical spread created by going long IBM January 260's for 7⅛ and shorting IBM January 280's for 2⅛ would have been bought at a debit of 5¾. Reversing the transactions would produce a 5¾ credit. If a spread is bought, the difference between the two premiums must expand if the investor is to profit. But if a spread is sold the difference must narrow. The increase or decline in the premium difference will depend on the movement of the underlying stock and the passage of time.

Vertical spread and calendar spreads can be designed to exploit either an increase in the price of the underlying stock or a decline. However, "bullish" vertical or calendar spreads generally possess better risk/reward characteristics than "bearish" spreads.

The theory behind both types of spreads emphasizes the sensitivity of time cost to expiration date and to strike price, two familiar relationships explained earlier.

In a bullish vertical spread, the investor hopes to replace time cost with intrinsic value in the long option with the lower strike price. As the stock advances toward the higher strike price of the short option, and the expiration date draws near, the time cost of the long option will become an increasingly smaller percentage of the total premium. The short option, however, will only reflect time cost, since the stock has

Market Makers and Floor
Brokers surround the Board
Broker at the CBOE.

193

not crossed the higher strike price. As expiration approaches, the time value of the short option will decline rapidly and, unless the stock goes above the strike price, the option will ultimately expire worthless. In practice, however, the price change of the underlying stock may be the predominant influence rather than disappearing time cost. Secondly, spreads are frequently closed out before expiration.

In late October, 1976, when IBM was selling at 256½, a bullish vertical spread could have been bought as follows:

Action	Option Series	Premium
Buy	January 260's	7⅞
Sell	January 280's	2⅛
		5¾ Debit

And, in late December, when the stock was 280, the spread could have been closed out at the following premiums:

Action	Option Series	Premium
Sell	January 260's	21⅜
Buy	January 280's	4⅞
		16½ Credit

This spread, then, gave the investor a gross profit of 10¾ (the difference between the 16½ ending credit and the 5¾ beginning debit) for a return of 87% on the 5¾ net investment before commissions and taxes. Of course, looking back, an investor can say it would have been more profitable to purchase the January 260 Call option alone. However, the point of spreading is to reduce the risk of a simple long or short position. By purchasing the spread for 5¾, the investor reduced the amount of capital at risk by nearly 30% from the 7⅞ premium of the single January 260 Call. And for this additional security, the investor accepted the certainty of a smaller reward.

With vertical spreads, both the maximum loss and the maximum theoretical profit at expiration can be determined from the outset. With bullish vertical spreads, the maximum profit is limited to the difference between the strike prices less the net premium paid. Should the underlying stock decline, the maximum loss would be the net premium paid. Thus, in the IBM spread the maximum gain could have been 14¼, the difference between 260 and 280, or 20, less the net premium paid of 5¾. Even if the underlying stock were to advance beyond the higher strike price the gain could not be greater than 14¼ because the loss on the short option would offset the gain in the long option. And, if the stock dropped below the lower strike, the loss could be no greater than 5¾ since both options would expire worthless. These profit and loss boundaries are illustrated graphically

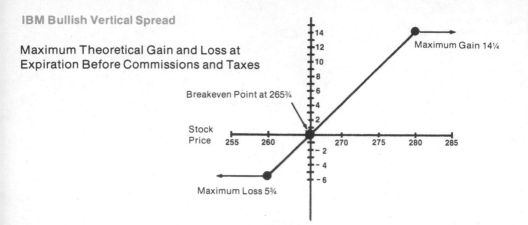

IBM Bullish Vertical Spread

Maximum Theoretical Gain and Loss at Expiration Before Commissions and Taxes

Maximum Gain 14¼

Breakeven Point at 265¾

Stock Price

Maximum Loss 5¾

above. In addition, the chart shows that this spread would "break even" at 265¾ which means that the long option must acquire 5¾ of intrinsic value to offset the opening debit.

In a bearish vertical spread, the option with the lower exercise price is sold and the option with the higher exercise price is bought. As a result, the maximum theoretical profit at expiration will be the net premium received and the maximum potential loss will be the difference between the exercise prices minus the net premium received.

In selecting a vertical spread, the investor should follow these guidelines:

(1) The underlying stock should be able to reach or exceed the higher strike price in a bullish vertical spread or a decline to or below the lower strike price in a bearish vertical spread.

(2) The debit, expressed as a percentage of the difference between the two strike prices, should be kept as small as possible in a bullish spread. The credit in a bearish spread should be as large as possible. Attractive percentages might be 30% or less for a bullish spread and 70% or higher for a bearish spread. In each spread, a lower debit or a higher credit, brings the breakeven point that much closer.

(3) Stocks selling for $50 or more should be considered first, since the difference between the premiums will be $10 or $20 and commissions will be lower than for stocks selling below $50.

The Calendar Spread

While vertical spreading emphasizes the interrelationships of stock price and strike prices (i.e., the vertical dimension of options), the theory of calendar spreading stresses the importance of time (the horizontal dimension of options). In a calendar spread, the investor first selects the appropriate strike price and then builds the spread by using two of the three expiration dates in whatever combination that produces the greatest reward. In most calendar spreads, one option with a closer expiration date is sold short and the other option with a more distant expiration date is bought long. Almost all calendar spreads will begin with a debit since the longer term option will always have a larger premium than the nearer term option. As time passes, however, the spread between the two premiums should widen allowing the investor to buy back the short option for significantly less while selling the long option for only slightly less than its purchase price.

The calendar spreader understands a simple fact of option valuation presented earlier, namely, that an option approaching expiration loses time cost far more rapidly than an option with several months of life remaining. This is particularly true for an expiring out of the money option, a condition dramatically illustrated on the chart of the expiring IBM January 280. The calendar spreader hopes the short option will share a similar fate.

A successful calendar spread might resemble the following example . . .

In late June, these quotations appear in the financial section of a local newspaper:

Option	Price	Jul	Oct	Jan	Close
KLM	60	1½	4	5	58¾

The investor, believing the underlying stock will remain relatively stable, buys a calendar spread for a debit of 1 by selling short an KLM Oct 60 at 4 and going long the KLM Jan 60 at 5. During the next several months, the stock has a series of small gains and losses but stays close to the strike price. Just before the October expiration, with the stock selling for $59, the October option is quoted at ½ while the January option is quoted at 3½ since it still has 3 months of remaining life. At this point, the investor successfully closes out the spread with a credit of 3. The investor's

initial $100 risk was able to produce a $200 gain (the difference between the closing credit and the beginning debit) even though the underlying stock remained steady. However, if the underlying stock had a large move either up or down, most likely the spread would have ended in the loss of nearly the entire debit. The spread must widen in a calendar spread, but as the stock moves further away from the strike price, the spread will narrow.

Calendar spreads should be appraised with the following requirements in mind:

(1) The underlying stock should be expected to trade in a narrow band slightly below or slightly above the strike price. The effect of large unexpected moves in the underlying stock will always be greater than the effect of diminishing time cost. As noted, large moves either up or down may force the spread into a loss.

(2) The short option should have a large "real" time cost which, again, will be found in the option with a strike price close to the price of the underlying stock.

(3) The initial debit should be small relative to a realistic projection of the spread's potential gain. In other words, it is ill-advised to risk an opening debit of say 4 if the spread's ultimate gain will be a net credit of 1.

196

Although vertical and calendar spreads can produce large gains, their effectiveness is hampered by three major drawbacks:

(1) **Commissions** A commission is paid every time an option is bought or sold. Opening and closing transactions on a typical vertical or calendar spread can, therefore, result in four commission charges. Even though commissions were excluded for simplicity in the examples of spreads just presented, the investor should always include this cost when computing any spread's potential gain or loss. In any spreading strategy, it is usually best to use several options. For example, the commission expense for five short and five long options should be proportionately smaller than only one short and one long.

Any spread that yields a gain only to have it eaten up by commissions is appropriately known as an "alligator" spread.

(2) **Volatility** Judging the short term price movement of the underlying stock is essential to the success of all option activity. Unfortunately, this is not as easy as it seems. Without knowing the volitility of the stock this task becomes even more difficult.

(3) **Exercise** The spreader may receive an exercise notice against the short option at any time. The probability of exercise increases as the underlying stock gains intrinsic value. Exercise radically alters the risk/reward ratio which was the basis for the spread's creation. It leaves the investor with a simple long position. Depending on the circumstances, the spreader may respond to an exercise notice by:

- Exercising the long call and delivering the stock.

- Delivering stock already owned.

- Buying stock in the open market.

- Delivering stock borrowed from the broker by shorting the stock and maintaining the long call as a hedge.

Hedging

Options can be used as a hedge to reduce risk in much the same way an insurance policy can provide protection against a catastrophic loss. If an investor owns stock and does not want to sell it, even though it may decline in the near future, a put option could be bought as a temporary hedge.

Investors should carefully review the tax consequences of any hedge beforehand. In certain instances, the holding period of the stock owned could be altered. Nevertheless, hedging a long position is sometimes worth considering.

The benefits of a short sale hedge involving the purchase of a call against an ordinary short sale position might be more compelling. The short seller is mainly concerned with the potential "unlimited loss" that could result if the price of the short stock were to soar. A short "squeeze" is particularly unnerving because additional capital is required when the stock is covered at higher prices — as opposed to owning a declining stock outright. Short sale hedging can be especially effective during a bear market when call premiums are usually depressed.

Puts and Calls Combined Often unpredictable corporate events place investors in a precarious position. They believe, or sense, that the price of a given stock is about to change substantially, but they do not know whether it will rise or fall. Such a situation might occur if a pending law suit is about to be resolved. If the company wins, its stock might increase sharply, but if it loses, the stock could drop precipitously. While many investors wait on the sidelines for the smoke to clear, a risk-conscious options investor might immediately use a strategy known as a "straddle."

A straddle consists of an equal number of puts and calls purchased or written simultaneously with identical strike prices and expiration dates. It enables the buyer to profit from a major price change in either direction while limiting the risk to the total combined premiums paid. Conversely, straddles produce substantial premium income for straddle writers who take the contrary view that the stock price will change little if at all.

Assume that the stock of the MNO Company has been trading steadily in early January at $50 a share awaiting certain corporate developments that could conceivably alter the price dramatically either up or down. An option buyer, convinced that a major price change will occur within the next three months, yet unsure of its direction, concludes that a straddle will be profitable. The MNO investor buys, simultaneously, an April 50 Call for 4 and an April 50 Put for 3½. By early April, the stock has advanced 20% to $60 a share. The call premium is now priced at 10½, while the put premium has fallen to ½. If the straddle is now "unwound," that is, terminated, through closing sale transactions, the options investor would have a $3.50 ($350) gross profit on the initial $7.50 ($750) investment as illustrated on the next page.

Depending on the amount of time remaining, it might be better to risk expiration rather than sell the put. It could regain some value if the stock were to drop suddenly.

Of course, the call could be exercised to acquire the stock which would then be sold to capture the profit. In practice, however, most straddles terminate in closing sale or purchase transactions.

If the stock had declined sharply instead of rising, the put would have been profitable, but not the call. A closing sale or exercise of the put would produce results virtually identical to those obtained from the profitable call.

This basic example provides the straddle buyer with several important guidelines:

(1) The total premium establishes the straddle's "breakeven points." The underlying stock must rise or fall by an amount equal to the combined premium before any profits can be realized. In the example above, the breakeven points were 57½ and 42½ because the initial premium was 7½ or 15% of the stock's price. The stock had to move at least 15% in either direction before the straddle was profitable. It is, therefore, important for the investor to keep the total premium as low as possible and the terms of the contracts realistic.

(2) A straddle involves "round trip" commissions on two options. As in other option strategies such as spreading and variable hedging, multiple commission charges must be computed accurately. Commission costs can easily turn a profitable trade into a loss. In addition, the investor should consult a tax advisor to anticipate the tax effects of any given trade.

(3) While the prospect of a double premium is enticing, a potential straddle writer should remember that a sharp move can produce a substantial loss. If the stock is not owned and it rises

MNO Company
Straddle

Bought			Sold			Profit/Loss	
April 50 Call	@	$4.00	April 50 Call	@	$10.50	Profit	+ $6.50
April 50 Put	@	$3.50	April 50 Put	@	$ 0.50	Loss	– $3.00
Total Premium			Total Premium			Total Gross	
	Paid	$7.50		Received	$11.00		Profit $3.50

sharply and the call is exercised, the writer would have to purchase the higher-priced shares in the open market. If the stock declines and the put is exercised, the investor might have to produce a large and immediate cash payment to pay for the put stock.

Puts and calls can be combined in several other ways to create various risk and reward strategies as in the "strip" — two puts and one call; or the "strap" — two calls and one put. These more exotic methods should be avoided until using individual puts and calls is thoroughly understood. Even then, each new idea should be scrutinized carefully with special emphasis on tax consequences, margin requirements, and commissions. The investor may find in some instances that simply buying or selling an unadorned put or call is more effective than creating the complex webbing of a supposedly advanced strategy.

Conclusion Options present a special
challenge. The investor must not only
judge *whether* a stock is going up or down
but *when* and roughly by *how much*.

As demonstrated, puts and calls can be
used in any type of market. They can be
used alone and in various combinations to
create numerous risk and reward opportunities. In the final analysis, however, successful option investing ultimately rests on
the accurate assessment of the underlying
stock's potential.

INDEX

ADDENDUM

Treasury bills may be purchased from each of the twelve Federal Reserve offices or from their branches. The necessary forms and other information may be easily obtained by writing or calling the nearest Federal Reserve facility. All are listed below.

A sample of the forms used, which may differ slightly from one region to the next, appears on the following page. When ordering the forms, be sure to specify "13-week," "26-week" or "52-week" maturity.

FEDERAL RESERVE OFFICES

OFFICES	ADDRESSES	TELEPHONE NUMBERS
Board of Governors	20th & Constitution Avenue, N.W. Washington, D.C. 20551	202-452-3000
ATLANTA	104 Marietta Street, N.W. Atlanta, GA 30303	404-586-8500
Birmingham Branch	1801 Fifth Avenue, North, P.O. Box 10447, Birmingham AL 35202	205-252-3141
Jacksonville Branch	515 Julia Street, Jacksonville, FL 32231	904-354-8211
Miami Branch	3770 S.W. 8th Street, Coral Gables, P.O. Box 520847, Miami, FL 31152	
Nashville Branch	301 Eighth Avenue, North, Nashville, TN 37203	615-259-4006
New Orleans Branch	525 St. Charles Avenue, P.O. Box 61630, New Orleans, LA 70161	504-586-1505
BOSTON	600 Atlantic Avenue, Boston, MA 02106	617-973-3000
Lewiston Office	Lewiston, MD 04240	207-784-2381
Windsor Locks Office	Windsor Locks, CT 06096	203-623-2561
CHICAGO	230 South LaSalle Street, P.O. Box 834, Chicago, IL 60690	312-322-5322
Des Moines Office	616 Tenth Street, P.O. Box 1903, Des Moines, IA 50306	515-284-8800
Detroit Branch	160 Fort Street, West, P.O. Box 1059, Detroit, MI 48231	313-961-6880
Indianapolis Office	41 E. Washington Street, P.O. Box 2020B, Indianapolis, IN 46206	317-635-4766
Milwaukee Office	304 East State Street, P.O. Box 361, Milwaukee, WI 53201	414-276-2323
CLEVELAND	1455 East Sixth Street, P.O. Box 6387, Cleveland, OH 44101	216-241-2800
Cincinnati Branch	150 East Fourth Street, P.O. Box 999, Cincinnati, OH 45201	513-721-4787
Columbus Office	965 Kingsmill Parkway, P.O. Box 189, Columbus, OH 43216	614-846-7050
Pittsburgh Branch	717 Grant Street, P.O. Box 876, Pittsburgh, PA 15230	412-261-7800
DALLAS	400 South Akard Street, Station K, Dallas, TX 75222	214-651-6111
El Paso Branch	301 East Main Street, P.O. Box 100, El Paso, TX 79999	915-544-4730
Houston Branch	1701 San Jacinto Street, P.O. Box 2578, Houston, TX 77001	713-659-4433
San Antonio Branch	126 East Nueva Street, P.O. Box 1471, San Antonio, TX 78295	512-224-2141

KANSAS CITY	925 Grand Avenue, Federal Reserve Station, Kansas City, MO 64198	816-881-2000
Denver Branch	1020 16th Street, Terminal Annex, P.O. Box 5228, Denver, CO 80217	303-292-4020
Oklahoma City Branch	226 Northwest Third St., P.O. Box 25129, Oklahoma City, OK 73125	405-235-1721
Omaha Branch	102 S. 17th St., Omaha, NE 68102	402-341-3610
MINNEAPOLIS	250 Marquette Avenue, Minneapolis, MN 55480	612-340-2345
Helena Branch	400 North Park Avenue, Helena, MT 59601	406-442-3860
NEW YORK	33 Liberty Street, Federal Reserve P.O. Station, New York, NY 10045	212-791-5000
Buffalo Branch	160 Delaware Avenue, P.O. Box 961, Buffalo, NY 14240	716-849-5000
PHILADELPHIA	100 North 6th Street, P.O. Box 66, Philadelphia, PA 19105	215-574-6000
RICHMOND	701 E. Byrd Street, P.O. Box 27622, Richmond, VA 23261	804-649-3611
Baltimore Branch	114-120 East Lexington Street, P.O. Box 1378 Baltimore MD 21203	301-539-6552
Charlotte Branch	401 South Tryon Street, Charlotte, NC 28230	704-373-0200
Charleston Office	1200 Airport Road, P.O. Box 2309, Charleston, WV 25311	304-345-8020
Columbia Office	1624 Browning Road, P.O. Box 132, Columbia, SC 29202	803-772-1940
Culpeper Office	Communications and Records Center, Federal Reserve Bank of Richmond, P.O. Drawer 20, Culpeper, VA 22701	703-825-1261
ST. LOUIS	411 Locust Street, P.O. Box 442, St. Louis, MO 63166	314-421-1700
Little Rock Branch	325 West Capitol Avenue, P.O. Box 1261, Little Rock, AR 72203	501-372-5451
Louisville Branch	410 South Fifth Street, P.O. Box 899, Louisville KY 40201	502-587-7351
Memphis Branch	200 N. Main Street, P.O. Box 407, Memphis, TN 38101	901-523-7171
SAN FRANCISCO	400 Sansome Street, P.O. Box 7702, San Francisco, CA 94120	415-544-2000
Los Angeles Branch	409 West Olympic Boulevard, P.O. Box 2077, Los Angeles, CA 90051	213-683-8323
Portland Branch	915 S.W. Stark Street, P.O. Box 3436, Portland, OR 97208	503-228-7584
Salt Lake City Branch	120 South State Street, P.O. Box 780, Salt Lake City, UT 84110	801-328-9611
Seattle Branch	1015 Second Avenue, P.O. Box 3567, Terminal Annex, Seattle, WA 98124	206-623-4320

FORM PD 4632-3
Dept. of the Treasury
Bur. of the Public Debt

TENDER FOR TREASURY BILLS
IN BOOK-ENTRY FORM AT THE
DEPARTMENT OF THE TREASURY
13-WEEK BILLS ONLY

FOR OFFICIAL USE ONLY
FRB Request No. _____
Issue Date _____
Due Date _____
Cusip No. 912793

MAIL TO:
☐ Bureau of the Public Debt, Securities Transactions Branch
   Room 2134, Main Treasury, Washington, D. C. 20226
☐ Federal Reserve Bank or Branch
   of your District at: _____

**BEFORE COMPLETING THIS FORM READ THE
ACCOMPANYING INSTRUCTIONS CAREFULLY**

Pursuant to the provisions of Department of the Treasury Circular, Public Debt Series No. 27-76, the public announcement issued by the Department of the Treasury, and the regulations set forth in Department Circular, Public Debt Series No. 26-76, I hereby submit this tender, in accordance with the terms as marked, for currently offered U.S. Treasury bills for my account. (Competitive tenders must be expressed on the basis of 100, with three decimals. Fractions may not be used.) I understand that noncompetitive tenders will be accepted in full at the average price of accepted competitive bids and that a noncompetitive tender by any one bidder may not exceed $500,000.

TYPE OF BID
NONCOMPETITIVE ☐   or   COMPETITIVE ☐   at: Price _____

AMOUNT OF TENDER $ _____
(Minimum of $10,000. Over $10,000 must be in multiples of $5,000.)

ACCOUNT IDENTIFICATION: (Please type or print clearly using a ball-point pen because this information will be used as a mailing label.)

Depositor(s) _____

SAMPLE ONLY

Address _____

PRIVACY ACT NOTICE
The individually identifiable information required on this form is necessary to permit the tender to be processed and the bills to be issued, in accordance with the general regulations governing United States book-entry Treasury bills (Department Circular PD Series No. 26-76). The transaction will not be completed unless all required data is furnished.

DEPOSITOR(S) IDENTIFICATION NUMBER

SOCIAL SECURITY NUMBER
FIRST NAMED ☐☐☐ – ☐☐ – ☐☐☐☐   OR   EMPLOYER IDENTIFICATION NO. ☐☐ – ☐☐☐☐☐☐☐

SOCIAL SECURITY NUMBER
SECOND NAMED ☐☐☐ – ☐☐ – ☐☐☐☐

DISPOSITION OF PROCEEDS

The par amount of the account will be paid at maturity unless you elect to have Treasury reinvest (roll-over) the proceeds of the maturing bills. (See below)
☐ I hereby request noncompetitive reinvestment of the proceeds in book-entry Treasury bills.

METHOD OF PAYMENT
TOTAL SUBMITTED $ _____   Cash $ _____   Check $ _____   Maturing Treasury Securities $ _____

DEPOSITOR'S AUTHORIZATION

Signature _____ Date _____   Telephone Number During Business Hours (_____)
Area Code

FOR OFFICIAL USE ONLY

Received by _____ Date _____

STATEMENT OF ACCOUNT		Issue Discount Price $		Amount of Discount $		
Date	Transaction	Par Amount Transacted		Account Balance	Authority Reference	Validation
		Decrease	Increase			
		$	$	$		

A: Department of the Treasury Copy

NOTES

NOTES

Understanding Wall Street

Credits

Pages   25, 27, 28, 33, 35, 36, 39, 41, 87, 126, 134 and inside front cover.
—photos courtesy of the New York Stock Exchange.

Pages   29, 30, 95, 180, 190
—photos courtesy of the American Stock Exchange.

Pages   99, 176, 192
—photos courtesy of the Chicago Board Options Exchange.

Page   196
—photo courtesy of the Philadelphia Stock Exchange.

Pages   64, 67, 69, 70, 72, 73, 75, 76, 77, 127
—illustrations reprinted with permission of The Wall Street Journal, copyright Dow Jones & Company, 1976. All rights reserved.

Pages   110, 113, 114, 116, 118, 121
—photos courtesy of Wide World Photos, Inc.

Pages   92, 140, 143
—photos courtesy of the Federal Reserve Bank of New York.

Page   130
—reprint courtesy of Financial Publishing Company of Boston, Mass.

Understanding Wall Street

What is a Share of Stock?
- Introduction
- The New-Design Chair Company
- The Importance of Profits
- The Stock Price
- Why Do People Buy Stocks?
- Dictionary of Wall Street Terms

Wall Street - How it Works
- Introduction
- Wall Street Defined
- A Short History
- The Primary Market
- The Secondary Market
- How the System Works
- Who Buys Stocks?
- The Future

Understanding Your Company
- Introduction
- Getting to Know the Company
- Financial Statements
- The Basics of Analysis
- Other Analytical Concepts
- Conclusion

Reading the Financial Pages
- Introduction
- The Dow Jones Averages
- The Stock Tables
- Stock Market Activity
- Market Breadth
- Earnings Reports
- Dividends and Stock Splits
- Short Interest
- The Interpretation of Business News

Investing and Trading
- Introduction
- Family Financial Planning
- The Stockbroker
- Discount Brokers
- Opening an Account
- Professional Counsel
- Investment Objectives
- The Margin Account
- "Playing" the Market
- Investment Clubs
- Investment Companies

Growth Stocks
- Introduction
- Why a Growth Stock?
- Measuring Growth
- Learning from the Past
- At What Price?
- Other Valuation Methods
- Perspective

Bonds, Preferred Stocks and the Money Market
- Introduction
- Bonds Explained
- Yields
- Calling
- Ratings
- Convertible Bonds
- Municipal Bonds
- Preferred Stocks
- U.S. Government Securities
- The Money Market

The Principles of Technical Analysis
- Introduction
- Bar Charts
- Chart Patterns
- The Dow Theory
- The Moving Average Deviation
- Beta
- Point & Figure Charts
- Technical Indicators
- Other Technical Observations

Stock Options
- Introduction
- Background
- Buying Options
- Writing Options
- Premium Valuation
- Reducing Risk
- Puts and Calls Combined
- Conclusion